THE ORGANIZED CHILD

Also from Richard Gallagher and Elana G. Spira

For Professionals

Organizational Skills Training for Children with ADHD:
An Empirically Supported Treatment
Richard Gallagher, Howard B. Abikoff, and Elana G. Spira

The
Organized
Child

**An Effective Program to Maximize
Your Kid's Potential—in School and in Life**

Richard Gallagher, PhD

Elana G. Spira, PhD

Jennifer L. Rosenblatt , PhD

THE GUILFORD PRESS

New York   London

Library of Congress Cataloging-in-Publication Data is available from the publisher.

ISBN 978-1-4625-2591-1 (paperback) — ISBN 978-1-4625-3249-0 (hardcover)

Contents

Part III
Organizational Skills for School Tasks

Part IV
Putting the Last Pieces in Place

Purchasers of this book can download and print a
supplementary appendix ("Creating Your Own Planner through
a Print Shop") and additional copies of select handouts and
forms at *www.guilford.com/gallagher2-materials* for personal
use or use with individual clients (see copyright page for details).

Preface

If you are picking up this book, odds are that you don't need to be sold on the importance of organizational skills for your child's school success (and for your family's harmony). There's a good chance you've sat up until the early hours with a panicked child trying to cram a month's worth of report writing into one night. You've likely banged on locked school doors long after the lights have been turned out, hoping someone can let you in to retrieve a forgotten but critically important book or paper. You may have resigned yourself to the nightly routine of texting classmates' parents to find out that day's homework. You've bought new organizational supplies; you've tried to teach your child new methods for organizing; you've probably lectured. And nothing has worked. You may have started to feel defeated, like you've become that nagging parent you never wanted to be. You probably feel pretty bad.

So let's spend the next few minutes making you feel worse.

(Stay with us, though. It may be a bit early for you to trust us, but the entire remainder of this book is dedicated to making you feel better—we promise!)

The bad news: This situation probably isn't going to get better on its own. We have been engaged in research for well over a decade with students who have organizational problems, and one clear finding is that these kids are different. While exposure to a few simple organizing tips and to some good modeling of organized behavior is enough to help most kids pick up sufficient organizational skills, a subset of kids have true difficulties in this area. Much in the same way some students may be brilliant in English but need remedial help in math, these kids are not able to develop organizational skills as easily as their peers.

The worse news: As these kids move through school, on to college, and into their careers, these problems are likely to become bigger and more significant. As they age, organizational demands and expectations increase, and whatever coping mechanisms they have developed to help them through will probably become less and less effective.

So now we move on to the good news, and we don't look back. The research program we have been involved with, under the direction of Dr. Howard Abikoff and Dr. Richard Gallagher, has been focused on understanding the exact kind of help these kids need to learn effective organizational skills. We have answers, and the purpose of this book is to share these answers with parents. We want to help you become the organizational skills coach your child needs.

Unlike many organizational programs on the market, this book is deeply rooted in hard science. It is based on the Organizational Skills Training (OST) program developed at the Child Study Center at New York University's Langone Medical Center, through one of the largest programmatic research efforts on organizational skills deficits in the world to date. This research focused on children with attention-deficit/hyperactivity disorder (ADHD), who often suffer from the most severe organizational challenges. Through close, repeated observation, we've identified a number of principles that are not typically part of the instruction on organizational skills given in schools, but that have worked particularly well for children with organizational deficits. You'll see these principles reflected throughout this book:

1. *Removing blame.* We look at organizational skills challenges as true skill deficits, not reflections of laziness or poor work ethic. We "externalize" these problems by placing blame on a series of characters we call "Glitches" (you'll read more about these later). Using this framework helps motivate kids by making the tone more positive and constructive.

2. *Turning long-term rewards into short-term rewards.* Kids with organizational skills deficits often have a style of thinking and behaving that favors short-term rewards over long-term rewards. We take advantage of this by putting short-term rewards in place for organized behaviors (for example, awarding a point for correctly writing down homework assignments in a given day) that would otherwise receive only long-term rewards (for instance, getting a good grade at the end of the semester because all homework was turned in).

3. *Taking one step at a time.* We recognize that organizing requires a large number of subskills (everything from keeping papers organized to

planning for a long-term assignment), and that even if a child is making improvements in one area, most of the attention usually goes to the area in which he's had his latest screw-up. We take one skill at a time, and focus on praising and encouraging that skill, regardless of what's going on in the areas we haven't tackled yet.

4. *Offering methods that work for these kids.* While a kid without organizational skills deficits may do fine with a complex system of sections and subsections in a three-ring binder, we focus on tools and routines that our research has shown to be effective for kids struggling with organization. These are usually things that are quick, simple, and easy to use.

5. *Practicing.* For other kids, you may be able to show them an organizational routine just once, but these kids need repeated practice—an essential component of our program.

Students who went through OST, the program based on these principles, showed significant gains in a wide range of outcomes. They had marked improvements in organization, time management, and planning as rated by both parents and teachers. They saw reductions in homework problems and increases in academic productivity and performance. And, in a finding that probably won't surprise anyone reading this book, these changes were accompanied by significant reductions in measures of family conflict. The OST program and the research on it are described in detail in our book for clinicians, *Organizational Skills Training for Children with ADHD*, and some of the forms and handouts in the present book are based on ones provided there.

This book is designed to teach parents how to guide their children through the essential components of this intervention. It is intended primarily for parents of 7- to 13-year-olds, because we have found that it is especially important to teach children organizational skills at a young age, to stop bad habits before they become ingrained. But you may find that your preteen doesn't always respond to instructions aimed at younger, elementary-school-age kids. We've modified the strategies presented in this book in our clinical work with older children, and we'll offer ways to use the material in more mature and collaborative ways, for preteens at the upper end of our designated age range and even for teens. While our research program was focused on children with ADHD, in our clinical work we have found these methods to be effective for students with organizational challenges stemming from a variety of causes.

The book is divided into four parts, which we suggest you read through in order before starting the program with your child. In Part I, we provide information to help you understand more about what organizational skills deficits are, why they occur, and why kids with these deficits need a specialized kind of help. (And, yes, we know this part sounds skippable, but we highly recommend you don't bypass it—because knowing why your child acts the way she does is incredibly useful in helping you guide her through the rest of the program effectively.) Part II gives you all the background information and describes the prep work you will need to do before launching into the program. Here you'll be introduced to important monitoring and motivational tools that are essential to the program. The heart of the program begins in Part III, where you will find a step-by-step guide to helping your child develop effective organizational skills and habits to help him with school and homework. You'll be using a planner that you can create yourself with a pocket folder and our forms, or can have bound at a copy shop. And Part IV shows you how to extend those skills to organizational challenges you may face with non-school-related tasks at home (such as cleaning up a messy bedroom or getting ready in the morning).

This program is not a quick fix by any means. There is a great deal of work prescribed for you and your child between these two covers. But the methods we offer you here are different from those you may have tried before. They are designed specifically to suit the brains of kids with organizational deficits, and they are backed by solid science. They have helped "hopelessly" disorganized kids become efficient and self-sufficient, and they have helped highly stressed families find a new state of calm. So we hope that as you and your child start in on this new challenge, you are feeling a little more optimistic.

Part I

Understanding Your Child's Disorganization

1

Organization and the Executive Assistant in Your Child's Brain

Among the many perks your child was granted upon his entry into this world was free use of a full-time executive assistant: you. You organized his toys, managed his social schedule, got him to doctors' appointments on time, and made sure he always had everything he needed when he needed it. As preschool rolled around, some small expectations may have been put in place for your child to use his own organizational skills—the time management of getting his shoes on before leaving for school, or the planned thinking required in gathering all the Legos he needed for his latest masterpiece—but for the most part, your role remained unchanged.

If you are reading this book, it is likely that your role as executive assistant continues to remain unchanged (or at least has changed less than you would like it to). The difference is that as your child got older, there were more expectations for her to develop organizational skills on her own— to use the executive assistant in her brain, rather than the one yelling reminders from the kitchen. And as your child's classmates slowly developed increasing independence in response to each of the demands placed on them, your child began to fall further behind. And you became more concerned, more frustrated, and more convinced that there was something different going on with your child.

The three of us are all parents, and so those feelings of concern and frustration are things we can easily relate to. But it was that third response—the idea that something developmentally different was happening here—that sparked our interest as clinical psychologists. We, along with our colleagues

3

at the Child Study Center at the New York University (NYU) Langone Medical Center, kept encountering kids who followed a similar pattern. These kids forgot to write down their assignments; lost their papers, coats, and lunchboxes; took hours to finish homework; and saved long-term work until the last minute. They weren't any different from their peers in their academic abilities—in fact, some were among the brightest we'd seen in our practice—but their grades usually didn't match their potential. And while many had been labeled lazy or lacking in work ethic, it was clear this wasn't the case. Most found organizing so difficult that they were putting in twice the effort for half the results. As clinicians charged with helping kids become their best selves, we wanted to find a way to help these students and their families. As researchers, we wanted to understand precisely what these difficulties were, why they occurred, and how to develop and test the best way to strengthen organizational skills in these children.

Thus began the Organizational Skills Training (OST) research program at the Child Study Center over 15 years ago, under the leadership of Dr. Howard Abikoff, a world-renowned clinical researcher who had spent the prior 30 years studying attention and behavior control problems. Each of us has been involved in various facets of the program over the past 15-plus years: Dr. Gallagher as a major collaborator in developing ways to measure organizational skills, creating the treatments upon which this book is based, and training therapists to implement the treatment; Dr. Spira as a clinician in the research trials and a coauthor of the manual for therapists; and Dr. Rosenblatt as a research clinician helping to adapt the elementary school treatment for use with middle schoolers. We have also all spent many hours working with children, teens, and their families in the Child Study Center clinical offices, using the lessons learned from the research program to help them develop skills in organization, time management, and planning.

These lessons, distilled and refined from our years of research and clinical work, are presented in this book. We'll talk more about the development of our program, the OST program, in a bit. But first let's start where the research program started all those years ago: taking a close look at what we know (and don't know) about the development of organizational skills in children.

How Organizational Skills Develop

When your child was in preschool, you may have been the major organizational force in your child's life, but at least you weren't alone. You could commiserate with other parents at the playground about the challenges of remembering to pack for show-and-tell on Thursdays, or tracking down a gluten-free, dairy-free, nut-free cupcake mix for the holiday party. But as children age, the expectation is for them to take more of these responsibilities onto their own shoulders. As your child moves through the grades, first-day-of-school instructions might look something like this:

■ **Third grade:** "For this year, you will get a list of the homework assignments at the start of the week. We'll put that list in your take-home folder, along with any handouts you need. Announcements will be e-mailed home."

■ **Fifth grade:** "We'll start using a planner this year. You will use your planner to write down your assignments, test dates, and due dates for projects. Today I'll teach you how to use your planner, and then every day from now on I will tell you what your assignment is and remind you to record it."

■ **Seventh grade:**

   □ *Social Studies:* "Today's assignment is to read Chapter 1 and answer the questions at the end of the chapter. Every other day you will find your homework listed in the box on the whiteboard."

   □ *Math:* "I've set up a class website. Check under the 'Section 3' tab every day to find your homework."

At home, a similar pattern of growing independence is typically taking place. Even the most organized young children rely on their parents for quite a lot: carefully scheduling playdates, extracurricular activities, doctors' appointments, and school obligations; packing lunchboxes and backpacks; and keeping drawers and closets stocked with weather-appropriate clothes and at least moderately organized toys. When children are very young (generally about seven years old or younger), even those who are developing organizational skills along a typical path cannot perform most of these actions on their own, without explicit instructions and lots of support from an adult. For example, you can usually teach a six-year-old to routinely put dirty clothes in a hamper (a one-step action), but most six-year-olds cannot independently perform an entire before-bedtime routine (bathe, put clothes in the hamper, get into pajamas, and brush teeth). As children begin to move into later childhood and the preteen years, though, many of these responsibilities begin to fall on their shoulders.

These increasing expectations, coupled with decreasing support from adults, are rooted in a fundamental educational concept called "scaffold-ing," based on the work of developmental psychologist Lev Vygotsky. Scaf-folding refers to a method of teaching in which teachers put strong supports in place when students are first developing a skill (analogous to the scaf-folding that supports a new building as it is being constructed), and then gradually remove these supports as the students become able to perform the skill independently.

Very little research has looked directly at how organizational skills typically unfold over time, but the patterns of scaffolding typically used by teachers give us good clues. The frameworks of increasing expectations tend to be largely similar across schools and classrooms, and are based on educa-tors' experiences of what the majority of children are capable of handling at each grade level.

In **elementary school**, teachers usually have begun expecting stu-dents to have their desks organized, to use their working time wisely, and to start planning and sequencing steps to complete tasks. Students typi-cally are responsible for having their books and homework with them when they arrive home from school, and for completing their homework without too much dawdling. Elementary school students need to keep track of the homework assigned each day. They are often also given their first structured long-term assignments, in which they are expected to spread work out over a few days.

By **middle school**, there is less "hand-holding" in regard to organiza-tion and time management. More often than not, students are expected to complete organizational tasks with no more help than a few brief reminders, while juggling homework and projects of increasing complexity.

And once kids hit **high school**, near-complete independence is expected for organizational functioning. Students are responsible for hav-ing everything they need on hand, for knowing their deadlines and their schedule, and for planning to avoid a last-minute rush on long-term assign-ments and tests.

At **home**, a parallel process is usually taking place. A child whose organizational skills are developing along typical lines moves from getting a jersey pulled over her head and cleats tied on her feet before being plunked into the car seat for soccer practice, to packing her own water bottle, shin guards, and ball and independently getting ready on time. She also begins to call friends herself to schedule sleepovers and check ahead of time for something good to watch together on Netflix.

But as you know all too well, this may be the pattern of development for *most* kids, but not *all* kids. In fact, you may be surprised (and possibly relieved) to know just how far from "all kids" it is: Our research has found that between 15 and 20% of children have deficits in organization, time management, and planning behaviors. So what is going on? Why are these kids different?

Executive Functions: The Operating System for Organizational Skills

Think back to any skills your child may have picked up pretty easily, without much help from the adults around him. Maybe he was singing along with the radio when other kids could barely manage "Mary Had a Little Lamb." Or maybe he figured out how to climb to the top of the monkey bars while others were still just tottering around, or was speaking in full sentences well before his peers. In any of these cases, he was likely born with particularly strong functioning in an area of his brain that helped that skill come more naturally to him. All children have different patterns of cognitive strengths, as well as areas of relative weakness where they need more support to develop their skills. For kids with organizational skills deficits, the most likely areas of weakness are problems with what we call "executive functions."

Executive functions are a collection of simple and complex brain activities we use to:

- Select goals for our actions, based on cues from our environment.
- Develop plans to reach those goals.
- Carry out those plans until the goals are accomplished.

A goal can be as simple as turning on a light, and the plan may be simply to get up, walk over to the light switch, and flip it on. Or it can be as complicated as figuring out how to get one kid to drama practice and another over to a friend's house and still make it to a work meeting on time, all mulled over while packing two lunches that don't contain any of the things your children have decided this week that they can't stand. More to the point, executive functions are at play when your child is remembering to look to the whiteboard for her homework assignment, organizing her room, or planning for a long-term assignment.

The executive functions have been found to be strongly related to life and school success. Children with strong executive functions have advantages in social behavior, in family relationships, in school, and in career success down the line. They know what tasks are important (filing an important paper in the correct folder before leaving class vs. getting to the hall as quickly as possible to hear the end of that funny story Dylan was telling); they know how to develop a plan to complete those tasks (doing a report a little bit each night vs. waiting to complete it in a crazed, Dr-Pepper-fueled all-nighter); they are flexible when they encounter unexpected challenges (calling a friend when an assignment is unclear vs. abandoning hope and retreating to the Xbox); and they stay focused on what they need to do to complete a task (working diligently until homework is done vs. "Hey— squirrel!").

The precise understanding of executive functions is still an active area of research, and there is much we still don't know. Over the past 50-plus years, scientists have proposed and debated a large list of possible executive functions, and they have yet to whittle down that list to an agreed-upon group. But there are six executive functions that are both generally accepted among researchers and have a clear link to organizational skills: attention control, inhibition, working memory, shifting, planning, and time management. These are described in the table on the facing page.

All six of these functions seem to improve with age, and generally in a predictable sequence. Attention control capacity emerges first, followed by inhibition, both of which tend to become mature during the preschool and early school years. Working memory abilities advance during the elementary school years and continue a more gradual advance into adolescence. The capacity for flexibly shifting actions emerges in late childhood and continues to grow in adolescence and adult years. Planning and time management are less well understood, but become more accurate in adolescence and adulthood. This pattern of development dovetails nicely with the common patterns of scaffolding for organizational skills we see in schools: increasing expectations for writing down assignments, for example, as working memory begins to develop; juggling of work from multiple classes, beginning when students become better able to shift tasks; and the introduction of more long-term work as planning skills emerge.

The Executive Office: The Frontal Lobes

This growth is all happening by means of a few developmental processes in the brain. Important areas of the brain are making new connections to one another; other connections that are not useful fall away; and increased

Executive Functions Related to Organizational Skills

Executive function	Definition	Practical reflection
Attention control	Controlling where, when, and on what elements of the environment attention should be focused.	Listening to a request from an adult instead of listening to the TV or music; looking at a blackboard lesson instead of the student in the next seat; paying attention to a teacher giving a homework assignment instead of daydreams about playing with a friend.
Inhibition	Stopping a nearly reflexive action in favor of a more appropriate action.	Waiting to raise a hand to answer a question instead of calling out; reading a word slowly instead of stating the word based on its first three letters; putting away books in a backpack instead of joining a conversation about a favorite video game.
Working memory	Holding some information in mind while completing another step in a task, and then bringing back the information from memory.	Remembering the meaning contained in the first part of a sentence while working to sound out a new word; recalling what paper is required for math homework while putting a pencil case in a backpack.
Shifting	Flexibly responding to the environment so that one set of actions is set aside for another set that is more appropriate because of a change in the environment.	Working to change where one walks when the path is blocked; setting aside work on a writing assignment to answer a question from a teacher; stopping a conversation to pick up an important paper that has fallen off the desk.
Planning	Selecting a goal, determining what steps are needed to reach the goal, and monitoring the effects of behaviors to see if the goal is closer to being reached.	Deciding how to complete a homework assignment; creating a plan for a book report; making and following a plan to have a playdate.

(continued)

Executive Functions Related to Organizational Skills *(continued)*

Executive function	Definition	Practical reflection
Time management	Knowing approximately how long different activities take to complete; keeping actions focused on the goal so time is not lost; and fitting actions into the known schedule.	Estimating how long it will take to get to basketball practice and leaving at the right time; starting homework early and completing it in time to eat dinner and watch a favorite show; spreading out the steps for a school presentation over several days so that it is not rushed.

efficiency in useful connections occurs as the brain matures. The site of most of this action is the "frontal lobe," the area of the human brain that is biggest as compared with the brains of other animals. Neuroscientists have been able to observe that the frontal lobes become more connected with themselves as well as with other essential brain centers during late childhood, adolescence, and adulthood. Those increases in connections are also associated with increases in behavioral, intellectual, and social development, including the executive functions. And the executive functions, in turn, are associated with the practical organization, time management, and planning skills that are the focus of this book.

But while we can describe the way an average brain develops, each child's brain is unique. And for some children, these connections may not be made as easily as for others.

So . . . Did You Just Tell Me That My Child's Brain Is Incapable of Organizing?

No! We told you that your child's brain may not develop organizational skills along a typical path, so the methods usually used to teach organization, time management, and planning in school may not be a good fit for her. The question then becomes: How do we teach organizational skills in a way that is accessible to these kinds of brains? And this was the question that sparked our research program.

You have slogged through a decent amount of science with us at this point. (Thank you!) If you are starting to nod off, we'll send you on your way with the short version of the rest of the chapter (we tested it; it works) and your official "hall pass": Proceed directly to Chapter 2. But if you have an interest in the research process that led to this book, or you'd like some data to sell you on all the hard work we are about to ask you to do, read on.

The NYU Organizational Skills Training Program

If you are still with us, you are a data nerd after our own hearts, so roll up your sleeves and let's get into the nitty-gritty.

When you want to try to solve a problem in a scientific way, the first thing you need to do is to make sure you have a way of measuring that problem. Otherwise, you have no way to gauge whether your solution is working. Fifteen-plus years ago, there was no reliable and valid way to measure organizational functioning. So Dr. Abikoff and Dr. Gallagher started by creating one.

The result was the Children's Organizational Skills Scales (COSS; Abikoff & Gallagher, 2009), a set of paper-and-pencil measures that used parent, teacher, and child ratings to establish where a child's organizational functioning fell in relation to the average student's. As part of the measure's development, the scales were administered to nearly 2,000 parents, teachers, and children. The primary purpose was to establish whether the measure was effective in reliably measuring organizational difficulties. But the data this generated also gave us a few insights into the nature of organizational deficits. One was that these deficits tended to group into three specific areas of functioning. For purposes of this guide, these areas can be described as follows:

1. *Using organized actions*: Use of organizational strategies and tools in order to keep aware of assignments and manage important items (such as using calendars, making outlines, and using folders).

2. *Lapses in memory and materials management*: Forgetting important information about assignments, losing important materials, or forgetting to pack needed items for homework.

3. *Task planning problems*: Failing to complete work on time, not getting to activities on time, and not knowing how to start, follow, or complete a plan.

As you can see in the table on the following page, each of these three areas of functioning requires several of the six executive functions.

Connecting Organization, Time Management, and Planning to Specific Executive Functions

Organizational skill	Situations	Executive functions required
Organization	**Tracking assignments and managing materials** • Recording assignments • Using calendars • Using checklists • Gathering, transferring, and storing papers, books, and other items • Clearing work spaces • Using lockers	• Attention control • Inhibition • Shifting • Working memory
Time management	**Fitting activities into a schedule** • Estimating time needed • Recalling appointments and schedules • Fitting activities into a schedule • Watching the passage of time • Speeding up or slowing down activity • Avoiding the impact of distractions on use of time	• Attention control • Inhibition • Shifting • Working memory • Time management • Aspects of planning
Planning	**Developing a plan and following it to completion** Selecting a goal Spelling out the steps for carrying out the goal Determining what materials and resources are needed for each step Estimating time for each step Fitting steps into the schedule Modifying the plan based on early results Checking that all steps are completed appropriately	• Attention control • Inhibition • Working memory • Shifting • Time management • Planning • Metacognition, or determining how to use certain thinking skills in carrying out a plan (as in, I need to pay attention to my math facts while I solve this problem)

The research on the COSS also gave us a better picture of those kids who tend to struggle with these organizational issues. These students were more likely to be:

- Younger.
- Boys.
- Children with learning disorders.
- Children with attention-deficit/hyperactivity disorder (ADHD).

Developing the Intervention

With the COSS in hand, the next step was to figure out how to take the kids who scored low on the scales and turn them into high-scoring kids. Since organizational deficits were so pervasive among children with ADHD, Dr. Abikoff and Dr. Gallagher focused on this population. Using both clinical wisdom and lessons learned from past research on elements that tend to be effective in clinical interventions in general, and in interventions for kids with ADHD specifically, they put together a program to teach students specific skills to meet the demands for *organization, time management,* and *planning* that children were most likely to face across a typical school day. They then began trying out the program, refining and adjusting in response to feedback from students, parents, and teachers. Ultimately, a few key elements were identified as being critical to understanding how to help students develop strong organizational skills:

- The day-to-day demands that were hampered by poor organizational skills fell into four practical areas: *tracking assignments, managing materials, managing time,* and *planning for long-term assignments.*
- Students needed frequent instruction and practice to make progress (clinical sessions were ultimately held twice a week).
- Students needed to learn one organizational skill at a time and not move on to the next until they had mastered the one they were working on.
- Students maintained motivation better when the adults helping them were patient, supportive, and positive.
- Children were better motivated for change when organizational problems were characterized as external challenges rather than internal deficits.

This last point is particularly important and worth a bit of elaboration. Too often, organizational problems are framed as character flaws: a lack of conscientiousness, work ethic, motivation. If one thing was clear from the early trials of the program, it was that this was not the case. Even kids who had internalized these messages, telling us that "I'm just lazy" or "I don't try," had actually spent significantly more effort over their lives trying (and failing) to become organized than their peers had. To address this feeling reported by so many of the kids we were working with—that something was "wrong" with them—Dr. Abikoff and Dr. Gallagher looked to successful treatments for problems like obsessive–compulsive disorder (OCD). These treatments used characters to represent the problem (such as an "OCD Monster") as a way of making it external. This borrowing resulted in one of the most novel aspects of the OST program: a series of characters called the "Mastermind" (the good guy, representing a well-functioning frontal lobe) and the "Glitches" (mischievous creatures that try to get kids in trouble with messages like "Don't write it down—you'll remember," or "You have plenty of time—do it later!"). We'll go into much more detail about these characters in Chapter 3.

The Moment of Truth: Testing the OST Program

After years of development, Dr. Abikoff and Dr. Gallagher were awarded a grant from the National Institute of Mental Health to conduct a five-year study evaluating the effectiveness of OST. Students with ADHD and significant organizational skills difficulties (as rated by parents and teachers on the COSS) were recruited for a randomized, controlled trial. "Randomized" means that they were randomly assigned to treatment groups: One group received OST; another group received an alternate treatment focused on training parents to provide behavioral rewards for organizational skill performance; and a third group was placed on a wait list to receive treatment after the evaluation period. Students were evaluated before the start of treatment and then one month after the end of treatment. To see if the effects of treatment lasted over time, students were reevaluated one month into the following school year and again four months later.

Students in the first two groups showed significant improvement over the wait-list group, although OST showed advantages over parent training on some specific outcomes and was preferred by parents offered a choice between the two. Students participating in OST scored significantly higher than their wait-listed peers on measures of:

- Organization, time management, and planning (from the COSS).

- Completion of schoolwork at school.

- Family conflict.

- Efficient completion of homework at home.

- Retention of benefits into the next school year.

After the large-scale trial was completed, smaller projects were undertaken to adapt and test the materials for middle schoolers. This book presents the essential elements of the original OST program, as well as extensions based on the middle school work, along with some of the most effective strategies from the parent training program. The program and the research based on it are described in our book for therapists, *Organizational Skills Training for Children with ADHD*, and some of the forms and handouts in the present book are based on ones included in that book.

We'll end this chapter with the happy news that, as your child's executive assistant, it is time to hand in your two weeks' notice. (OK, maybe a bit more than two weeks, but still, your days are numbered.) We are now embarking on recruiting and intensively training a new executive assistant for your child—the one parked right up there in her frontal lobe.

2

From Parent to Coach

*Taking on a New Mindset
to Get Your Child Organized*

At the risk of sounding as though we've promised too much in Chapter 1, it is time for us to admit that the process of handing over the job of executive assistant from you to your child is a slow and gradual one. It's also one in which you will be involved significantly: The task of getting your child organized will probably require *more* effort from you than you currently expend in just doing things for him. But it is a (relatively) short-term investment toward a long-term reward: a more self-reliant, self-sufficient kid.

And we know that's a lot to ask, because you are probably already doing a lot more work to organize your kid than you'd like to, and a lot more than you see the parents around you doing. As we've discussed in Chapter 1, as children grow older, they are increasingly capable of carrying out complex actions requiring organization, time management, and planning. But as your child grew, her struggles with these types of tasks likely became apparent, and many times it probably felt like it was easier to keep doing them yourself than to go through the struggle of handing them over. And thus your role as executive assistant became entrenched. Often these roles and habits have become so familiar (and the memories of the battles that may have occurred are still so fresh) that it can take a mental leap to really get going on the process of change.

The point of this program is to offer you a *different* approach to helping your child—because, frankly, if the traditional methods had worked for your child, you probably wouldn't be here reading this book. And trying a different approach will require some important shifts in mindset. In this chapter we'll introduce you to some new ways to approach your child's disorganization.

An important note before you dig in: This chapter is meant to be an *introduction* to these concepts. Your real plan of action begins in Part II, where we begin to walk you, step by step, through how to use the concepts to implement the program. So even if you are chomping at the bit, don't use this information to get started on making any changes yet. We promise we will get there!

OK, so here's how to start:

1. *Increase expectations.* First, you will probably need to stop doing as many things *for* your child as you have been doing to this point. For example, your eight-year-old should be capable of picking out a snack and packing it, with a water bottle, in his bag each evening. Similarly, your nine-year-old should be able to put her homework assignments back in the correct folder each evening, instead of leaving them on the kitchen counter and running off to play. If your child knows that you will do these things for him, he will be less likely to try to do them on his own. In Part III we will walk you, step by step, along a path to setting new expectations one at a time. But if you find yourself saying, "I'll skip this skill; it's easy enough for me to keep doing it on my own," take a minute to stop and rethink. Your child's independence is a valuable goal, for both your sakes.

2. *Provide support.* While you want to start slowly to increase expectations for your growing child, you don't want to withdraw all support overnight or withdraw it in a punitive manner. Remember our discussion in Chapter 1 of teachers' use of scaffolding—supporting children while they need it, and then removing supports gradually and planfully? This works just as well at home as it does at school. You can let your child know that because she is getting older and more responsible, you believe that she can start doing some of the tasks that you have been doing for her. Then tell your child which concrete steps she will now be expected to do, and let her know that you are available to help, if needed. For instance, you might say, "Before you go to bed each night, please pick one snack from this cabinet, fill your water bottle, and put both items in your backpack. If you need my help unscrewing the top from the water bottle, I'll be happy to do that." When your child performs an organizational task independently, praise her for taking more responsibility.

3. *Monitor.* Your child may not pick up on these new routines as quickly as you expect. For some children, increasing expectations and providing

clear prompts and praise will do the trick. However, for a child who has weaker organizational skills, you may need to provide more explicit, guided instruction and use behavior management strategies to motivate mastery, especially when it comes to school-related tasks. If this is the case for your child, do not fear—Parts II, III, and IV of this book outline a plan that will help you and your child work together on becoming more organized.

 Tip for Older Children

If your child is already in middle or high school and struggles with organiza-tion, you may feel even more frustrated with the lack of independent func-tioning in this area. Your frustration is completely understandable—but try not to let it guide the way you address this issue with your preteen or teen. You may be tempted to simply stop helping and let your teen suffer the consequences—and, in some situations, that "tough love" approach might work. For example, you may find that if you stop putting your preteen's iPad in his backpack each morning, and your child gets in trouble with his teacher for not having it in class, he will be more likely to remember it in the future. However, this approach will probably not work for some older children who have true deficits in organizational skills. For these children, forcing them to "sink or swim" may backfire—because they're not just going to learn how to "swim" as if the instructions were already ingrained. If your child is in this group, you really need to teach her to swim. For her, following the three steps for moving toward more independence will be essential in helping her grad-ually make changes.

Remember That Executive Functions Are Needed Everywhere

Consider this scenario (which probably happens in your home more often than you would like): As you're tucking your eight-year-old son into bed, you remind him that he has band practice in school the next day and should take his flute to school. The next morning, at about 10:00 A.M., you get a call from your son at school, begging you to bring him the flute that he left in his room. You recognized that this is hard for him and gave him a reminder. Why wasn't this enough?

It will be important as you work through this program to think con-stantly about the hidden executive skill gaps that may be tripping up your child, even on tasks that may seem easy. For children who struggle with organization, a verbal reminder is not always enough, especially if that reminder is not given in the immediate situation when action is required. For the boy in this example to succeed, he would have to use strong working memory skills: He would have to hold your verbal reminder in his memory overnight, recall that reminder the next morning, and use that information to motivate concrete action (putting the flute in his bag). While these steps might seem simple to an adult who is able to use working memory efficiently, they are incredibly complex for children with weak executive functioning. For these children, telling them to do something is simply not enough.

Behavior Change Is Hard Work for Kids

While your child might recognize that forgetting important items or neglecting to hand in assignments is not an appropriate behavior, she probably does not know *how* to carry out the actions necessary to organize herself, given her still-developing executive functioning skills (see Chapter 1). Your child will need time and extra support from you to learn to use a new organizational routine consistently. You might think it's a simple step to pack up the homework materials after finishing nightly assignments, but your child may struggle to remember this step without a reminder. Furthermore, most children have a hard time understanding the long-term consequences of their actions. Your child sees a backpack that isn't packed or a pencil box that is running low on materials. You see the poor grade that the child will get if he doesn't hand in his homework consistently, or the problems that will occur when your child doesn't come to class prepared with his materials. Your child may have real difficulties mentally connecting short-term behaviors to their long-term consequences.

Organization is not an innate ability that naturally emerges in children (or adults). Organizational skills must be taught and practiced to become automatic, just like your child must learn how to decode words and add numbers before she can become proficient in reading or math. Acquiring the basic skills that are necessary for organization may not come easily to your child, just as some children have more difficulty understanding why $10 - 2 = 8$. If you tell a child who struggles with math to "just try harder," or get frustrated or punish her when she can't complete a math assignment that she doesn't understand, that child is unlikely to get any better at math. The same is true for a child who has difficulty being organized: The child

needs a chance to learn and practice the building blocks that lead to organized behavior, and needs you to support her as she attempts to master this
difficult new skill area.

A Telling-and-Doing Program

For these reasons, the program outlined in this book is not a *telling* program;
it is a *telling-and-doing* program. You do give your child verbal explanations
and suggestions (the telling), but you also provide the necessary support for
the child to put what you just told him into practice—the doing. As you
work through this book, you will feel more confident telling your child about
tools or routines that can help him become more organized—for example,
suggesting that he use an accordion file instead of individual folders to file
papers. However, these suggested steps are only one piece of the puzzle and
will get you only so far without the second piece—your active support in
motivating your child to practice and integrate those new skills and routines
into his life. OST is based on behavioral principles of change. Simply stated,
you need to break down each behavioral objective into its concrete, component parts; provide ample opportunities to practice each specific part; and
motivate continued performance of the desired behavior(s) with praise and
rewards. Let's break that process down a bit more specifically:

Teach by breaking it down. First, you will teach your child a specific
routine—for example, packing her backpack after she finishes her homework. You will not assume that your child knows *how* to pack her backpack;
instead, you will break down this routine into essential steps and demonstrate how each step is carried out. We outline steps for teaching organization, time management, and planning in Part III, so you don't have to make
this part up! For example, if you are teaching your child to break down the
backpack-packing routine, you will point out the essential steps: "Put all
your papers back into the correct folders, and then place all the folders in
the backpack. Add a snack and a water bottle. Now check that you have
everything you need: Did you leave any papers on or under the table? Have
you considered other things (such as library books that may need to be
returned, instruments for band practice, or gym clothes)? Finally, zip up the
backpack, and leave it by the front door."

Practice. Next you will have your child practice this routine while
you observe, praising the things she does well ("You remembered to check

your folders for all the papers you need!") and pointing out things to try again ("Did you think about what specials you have tomorrow?"). You may need to practice a few times before your child gets the hang of it. In Part III, we give you some tips for making sure these practice sessions go smoothly.

Prompt, monitor, praise, and reward. This is the most important part of the process, and one to which we dedicate an entire chapter (Chapter 5). If you stop after the teaching and practice phases, and expect that your child "got it," you will be sorely disappointed by the results: Your child may remember the steps for the next day or two, but is likely to slip right back into old patterns fairly quickly. You will need to follow through by prompting your child to use the new skill/routine each day, monitoring your child's progress in a formal way, and praising and rewarding your child for using the skill/routine. Children with weak organizational skills will not be able to master new routines without timely prompts and increased motivators from parents and teachers.

"What If I'm Not Organized Enough to Teach My Child Organization?"

Often we speak with parents who blame themselves for their children's disorganized habits: "How can I expect my kid to get ready in the morning on time when I'm late picking her up at school almost every day?" or "It's no wonder my child loses his planner all the time; it's impossible to find anything in our house!" Our advice to parents with these concerns is, first, to drop blame from the equation, because that is never a productive place to start! However, it may be useful to examine your own organizational habits and think about whether small changes in the home environment could help support your child's organization. You might want to consider the following questions:

■ *Is a calendar posted somewhere in the house where my child can view the schedule for the week?* Many parents find that keeping a large calendar can help everyone keep track of after-school activities, playdates, doctors' appointments, and the school day schedule (for those schools that operate on a rotating six-day schedule).

■ *Can I organize the "stuff" in my house more efficiently?* Chapter 11 provides some suggestions for how to get stuff under control by using storage containers and bins. If you think that the "stuff" in your house might get in the way of setting up more organized systems related to schoolwork (for example, if you can't find a good homework spot for your child because every room is overrun with her younger brother's toys), it might be a good idea to preview Chapter 11 and see if you can get the mess under control first. One mom shared a simple solution with us that worked wonders in her house: She bought a rolling cart with file folders and bins, and assigned each child file folders for artwork and important papers; the bins held writing, drawing, and art supplies. Of course, she had to make sure that the kids learned routines for filing the papers and putting materials back on the cart—but after a short time there were no more piles of papers on the kitchen table, and everyone had the necessary materials for homework and art projects, no matter where each child chose to work.

■ *Is there a clock in every room where my child needs to do schoolwork or get something done in a timely manner (such as showering and getting dressed)?* We discuss how to help improve your child's time management skills in Chapter 9, and the use of a clock is an important piece of all the suggested routines.

■ *Do I need to shift the schedule slightly to make it more likely that my child can get things done on time?* For example, if the morning school bus comes at 8:15 and you wake everyone up at 7:45, you might have trouble getting everyone out the door with what each child needs on time. Consider all the times during the day when you find yourself rushing (and probably yelling), and think about whether there is a way to shift the schedule a bit to minimize stress and maximize success.

■ *Do I model a planful approach to tasks for my kids?* Chapter 10 outlines steps for helping your child plan for larger tasks. As you read that chapter, think about how you might be able to model that process for tasks that you have to complete every day. Is your mom's birthday coming up? Talk to your child about the things you need to do to be ready with a gift and celebration for Grandma. Are you planning a holiday dinner? Ask your child to help you come up with a menu and grocery list. You use organizational skills on a regular basis, so the more you can start actively modeling those skills for your child—that is, pointing out what you're doing, and demonstrating appropriate steps—the more likely it is that your child will use those skills.

Don't worry if your first answer to some of the questions above is "no." Throughout the book, we provide tips that we have developed from work with parents and children that will help you carry out the steps in the program. As you read the chapters that follow, you will work on ways to improve not only your child's organizational skills, but also the organization of your home environment. Remember to cut yourself some slack if you don't follow through perfectly—every new system will have its stops and starts!—and then think about what you need to do differently to achieve a better result. For example, if you find that you often forget to prompt your child or give a reward for using an organized routine (a process we describe in Chapter 5), think about how you can remind yourself to do so. Perhaps you need to post the list of skills that your child is working on in a more vis-ible location (on the refrigerator door, for instance), and set a specific time each evening to review what she earned points for and to give a reward. Give yourself and your child some time to adjust to this new way of doing things. (If you find that your efforts fall short, you can seek some profes-sional guidance, as there are several books and programs for enhancing organized actions in adults. See the Resources list near the end of the book.)

Remember that you are your child's first and most important teacher. So settle in and prepare for the first round in your professional development as an organizational coach. Part II will give you the inside information that you'll need to start training your child to take control of organization, time management, and planning.

3

Discovering Your Child's Organizational Strengths and Weaknesses

Ten-year-old Brandon and his mother are meeting with the school guidance counselor, who has noticed that Brandon is falling behind in his schoolwork. The guidance counselor begins the conversation by gently asking Brandon why he thinks he has missed so many homework assignments. Brandon slumps down farther in his chair and mumbles, "I only missed a few." His mom immediately interjects, "A few?? Your teacher sent home a note saying that you only handed in one of your math sheets for the past week, and you haven't completed a reading log in three weeks! You're completely irresponsible." Brandon simply shrugs and stares out the window as his mom continues, "Half the time, I don't even know what his assignments are! He never fills out his planner, and even when he does, he always forgets to bring his books home. Come on, Brandon, you have to admit that you're completely disorganized." Brandon responds, "All my friends forget homework every now and then. It's not such a big deal."

Brandon's refusal to admit his organizational difficulties is fairly typical and even has a name: "positive illusory bias." What this means is that, despite clear evidence of weak organizational skills, many children simply don't see (or don't admit that they see) these problems. Ironically, this bias is particularly common in the children who struggle most with organizational skills—children diagnosed with ADHD. In our work with numerous children, children's own reports of their organizational skills are consistently more positive than their parents' or teachers' reports. It has been suggested that this denial of problems is self-protective: If children don't recognize their limitations, they don't have to feel bad about them.

Although your child may not see a problem with her organizational abilities, you may notice that certain areas related to organization are consistently difficult for her. We suggest that you take several steps to set the stage for positive change in your child's organizational abilities.

Getting More Information: Your Child's Organizational Strengths and Weaknesses

To determine which specific organizational difficulties you would like to help your child improve, you may complete the Organization, Time Management, and Planning (OTMP) Inventory on page 26. (See the box at the end of the Contents list in the front of the book for information about printing a copy.) You can complete this list of questions by yourself, or with your spouse or partner, before speaking with your child. Think about the tasks that your child must complete on a typical school day—getting ready in the morning, taking all needed items to school in the backpack, being prepared for lessons with the appropriate materials, bringing home materials for homework, completing homework, doing chores, and getting ready for bed. What are some typical challenges that your child faces in completing these tasks? Are there areas that are constant sources of conflict within the home, or ones that the teacher reports are consistently problematic in school? If you find that you've checked the "Often" or "Always" column for a number of behaviors, it's a good idea to discuss these problems with your child and come up with a plan for improving skills in the identified areas.

As you complete the OTMP Inventory, you'll notice references to four types of "Glitches." We'll explain those next.

Establishing a Useful Mindset: Introducing the Glitches

In our work with children and their families, we have found it helpful to frame problems with organization, time management, and planning

Organization, Time Management, and Planning (OTMP) Inventory

Observations	Never	Sometimes	Often	Always
Tracking assignments (Go-Ahead-Forget-It Glitch)				
My child writes down assignments inconsistently				
My child forgets to take things he/she needs to school.				
My child forgets about assignments that are due the next day.				
My child often arrives at school and finds out there is a test that he/she didn't know about or forgot about.				
Managing materials (Go-Ahead-Lose-It Glitch)				
It is hard for my child to find the papers he/she needs.				
My child arrives home without papers/books needed for homework.				
My child forgets completed assignments and/or other necessary materials at home.				
My child's backpack is messy.				
My child's desk is messy.				
My child misplaces personal belongings (such as gloves, sweatshirts, small toys, electronics).				
Time management (Time Bandit)				
My child has difficulty getting started with homework on time.				
My child takes a long time to complete homework.				
My child needs constant prompts to get ready in the morning.				
My child has difficulty completing daily routines (such as tidying up the bedroom, showering, doing small chores) in a timely manner.				
Task planning (Go-Ahead-Don't-Plan Glitch)				
My child has trouble knowing how to start projects/assignments.				
My child has difficulty breaking down larger projects into steps.				
My child has to rush to complete long-term projects, due to lack of planning.				
My child often hands in work that is incomplete and/or messy.				

(abbreviated from here on as OTMP) as being due to "Glitches" in the brain. This is why we've included mentions of these Glitches in the OTMP Inventory. We present these Glitches as mischievous little creatures who hang out in everyone's brain and try to trip up the "Mastermind," who is in charge of getting things done. For example, the Go-Ahead-Forget-It Glitch might tell your child that it is not necessary to write down his assignments, because he will remember them when he gets home. When the child gets home and can't remember the assignments, the Glitch laughs, knowing that it's thwarted the Mastermind again and gotten the child into trouble.

This model is our way of explaining the executive functions (and the difficulties some people have with executive functions) in a child-friendly, nonthreatening manner. We've found that children react quite positively to the idea of troublesome Glitches that are trying to trip them up. This idea allows you to talk to your child in a neutral way about problems that result from being unprepared, losing an important handout, or missing the school bus. It also promotes adult–child collaboration: We encourage children to team up with their parents and teachers to "beat" the Glitches so that the Mastermind stays in control.

We suggest that you read through our Guide to the Glitches handout first on your own, to get a sense of how to think about the different problems that many kids face with organization. (The Guide to the Glitches begins on the following page. See the box at the end of the Contents for information on printing a copy to keep handy.) After completing the OTMP Inventory, you should have a better sense of which Glitches are most troublesome for your child (we've organized the Inventory by Glitch, to help with this process). You can then read through the Guide to the Glitches with your child (it's written to speak directly to your child, so older kids can read it themselves) and talk about the descriptions of how the different Glitches interfere with the Mastermind and cause problems. We have found that kids respond best when their parents can come up with examples of when particular Glitches have gotten them in trouble. If you've ever put your keys down in an odd spot and spent an hour searching for them, blame it on the Go-Ahead-Lose-It Glitch. Tell your child about the time the Go-Ahead-Forget-It Glitch got you and you forgot a really important meeting with your boss, or the way the Time Bandit steals your sleep time by convincing you to spend an hour watching TV instead of getting your chores done. Children love to hear about how their parents have "messed up"; this gives the adults license to admit that they too may struggle with Glitches.

The next section of this guide includes details about each Glitch. When we work on new skills, we'll review it so we know how to beat the Glitches!

HELPING YOUR MASTERMIND WIN!

The Mastermind.

It takes brains to do everything we do: breathing, eating, even sleeping. Of course, it takes brains to learn and go to school. Walking into the building, finding your class, saying "Hello" to your friends, reading, and listening to your teachers all take brains. We can think of our brains as having different parts that help us do different activities. There are also parts that help us stay organized. These parts help us look around and figure out what we have to do. These parts work together to let us know what steps we have to take to brush our teeth, make a sandwich, or get ready to go to the movies. Let's think of these organizing parts of our brains—the parts that help us decide what to do and how to do it—as acting together like a sort of superhero, and let's call this hero the Mastermind. The Mastermind helps us control our actions.

    The Mastermind is outstanding, but not perfect. Sometimes the Mastermind is not active enough. When you are tired or nervous or rushing around, the Mastermind does not work so well. For some people, keeping the Mastermind active enough is

(continued)

really difficult. Others might say that that these people are careless or lazy. But that is **not true**.

Experts have learned that small, annoying problems develop when the Mastermind is not active enough. Your brain is more likely to make mistakes, and when that happens, Glitches get in the way. We all have Glitches creeping around in our brains. They mess us up by telling us silly things or making us forget to use skills that keep us organized and get things done. Have you ever forgotten a book or paper that you needed to take to school? If you have, that was the Glitches' work. Have you ever lost an important paper, like your homework or a special permission slip? That was also caused by Glitches. Every time we slip up and make mistakes, the Glitches throw a party. They love it when we are not in control of our actions.

Experts have put together some tips and tricks that can help you train the Mastermind to be more active, so you can control the Glitches. This program will teach you some new habits, so you know which steps to use to keep the Mastermind in control and stop the Glitches from making mischief. Let's find out about four naughty Glitches.

First, there is the **Go-Ahead-Forget-It Glitch.** This Glitch doesn't want you to remember important things, like homework assignments, important books that you need to bring home to study for a test, or the chores that your mom or dad asked you to do. It tricks you and tells you that you don't have to write down your homework or check to see if you have everything with you when you leave school. This Glitch *wants* you to forget things and get into trouble. When it wins, you look silly, because you don't have the right things with you or you don't know what you need to do.

There is also the **Go-Ahead-Lose-It Glitch.** This Glitch takes your mind off your things, so you misplace them or lose them. It tells you that you will find important papers no matter where you put them, so it convinces you to just stuff papers into your backpack or desk instead of using a folder. When you can't find your homework even though you did it, or you can't find your iPad because you leave it in a different place each time you use it, the Go-Ahead-Lose-It Glitch has gotten you.

The **Time Bandit** is the Glitch that makes you lose track of time and forget when things are due. If you ever remembered a big school project the night before it was due, this Glitch was around. This Glitch convinces you that you can do things later, without planning a schedule. The Time Bandit is also around when you find that you did not get your homework done, even though you had several hours to do it. It confuses you, and it distracts you while you're working, so that you don't use your time well.

Finally, the **Go-Ahead-Don't-Plan Glitch** takes away your good thinking skills. This Glitch tells you that you don't have to plan, which means you don't have to think ahead about the steps needed to complete big tasks. If you've ever handed in an assignment that was missing important parts, or found you don't enjoy a playdate as much because you forgot to plan which toys and games you wanted to bring, you've had trouble with this Glitch.

(continued)

GO-AHEAD-FORGET-IT GLITCH

This Glitch lurks in your memory and wipes out things you should remember or prevents you from remembering things.

Some Things the Go-Ahead-Forget-It Glitch Might Say

"Don't worry, you won't forget to take home your math book. You can pack it later, after you go to recess."

"You'll remember what the homework is without writing it down."

"You don't have to use a calendar to keep track of tests or projects. Your teacher will remind you when those are due."

When Is the Go-Ahead-Forget-It Glitch Around?

This Glitch often shows up when your teacher tells you what the homework assignments are for the day. It also shows up when you are packing up your things and keeps you from being careful about remembering what things to take with you. Then, when you get home and don't have the materials you need to complete your homework, this Glitch throws a party.

The Go-Ahead-Forget-It Glitch.

(continued)

GO-AHEAD-LOSE-IT GLITCH

This Glitch gets into the parts of your brain that control what you do, and it convinces you to put things away in the wrong place or in a place you will forget. It tricks you into misplacing your things, so that you come to school without your homework or get home without your books or papers. This Glitch makes you lose parts of your toys and makes it hard for you to find things. It also makes your backpack and desk really messy.

Some Things the Go-Ahead-Lose-It Glitch Might Say

"Hurry up! We have to do something else. Just drop that toy over there, and you can put it away later."

"Let's go watch TV. You can put your homework in your backpack when you're done."

"Just put that homework worksheet into your desk. You'll find it later."

"Even if you lose your iPad, Mom or Dad will help you find it."

When Is the Go-Ahead-Lose-It Glitch Around?

This Glitch shows up whenever you are given a paper at school, and when you are packing up at the end of the school day. It hangs out whenever you open your backpack, especially when you take things out; it might distract you, so that you forget to put things back in the right spots. When you are done playing, the Glitch tells you to just rush to the next activity without putting away your stuff. The Glitch is very happy when you can't find something important.

The Go-Ahead-Lose-It Glitch.

(continued)

THE TIME BANDIT

The Time Bandit gets into the parts of your brain that keep track of time. This Glitch convinces you not to worry about clocks or calendars. It confuses you, so you don't keep track of how much time you have to do things.

Some Things the Time Bandit Might Say

"Take it easy. We can take all the time we want to do this work."

"Don't worry about what time it is; your mom or dad will make sure you get to school on time."

"It's OK to take a little break from your homework and make a paper clip chain. You have plenty of time to get this done."

When Is the Time Bandit Around?

It's OK if the Time Bandit takes over when you are on vacation or relaxing on weekends; everyone needs a break from worrying about schedules. But the Time Bandit can also show up during homework time or other times when you have to meet a deadline (like getting to soccer practice by 5 P.M.). That's when the Time Bandit causes problems, because it slows you down and keeps you from being ready on time. The Time Bandit may also try to trick you into thinking that you can wait to start projects. This Glitch takes the Mastermind's eyes off the clock and the calendar, and that's how it gets you into trouble.

The Time Bandit.

(continued)

GO-AHEAD-DON'T-PLAN GLITCH

The Go-Ahead-Don't-Plan Glitch gets into the parts of your brain that control your thinking. This Glitch convinces you not to think ahead or think about the steps needed to complete a task or activity. This Glitch may trick you into believing a project is easy and doesn't require planning or can be started at the last minute.

Some Things the Go-Ahead-Don't-Plan Glitch Might Say

"Why bother planning how you will do this science project? Mom and Dad always do the planning for you."

"You don't need to think about the materials you need for this project. I'm sure you already have everything."

When Is the Go-Ahead-Don't-Plan Glitch Around?

Sometimes it's great just to relax and not plan your time. But when you find yourself cramming to do a project at the last minute, this Glitch has been in control. Sometimes this Glitch works with the Go-Ahead-Forget-It Glitch and the Time Bandit. It can tell you not to worry about what materials you need for homework or not to think about the steps you have to take to get ready. This Glitch loves it when you get scolded for rushing, handing in sloppy work, or forgetting to do something until the last minute.

The Go-Ahead-Don't-Plan Glitch.

Tip for Older Children

If your child might see the full Glitches model as immature, you can use the alternate Guide to the Glitches for Teens (see page 35), which presents the concepts in a more mature way. (Again, information about printing a separate copy is provided at the end of the Contents.)

Reading through the Guide to the Glitches with your child should set the stage for an initial conversation about how the Glitches are making it difficult for the Mastermind in your child's brain to be in control. Below we suggest some ideas for making this conversation as positive and constructive as possible.

Setting the Right Tone for an Open Discussion

It is quite likely that your child may not be thrilled when you start to put together a laundry list of his organizational weaknesses. (Think about how you feel when a know-it-all colleague points out why her system for keeping track of sales or writing up memos is so much more efficient than yours, or when your spouse calls you out for leaving your shoes in the middle of the floor!) Remember that your child's self-image, when it comes to organizational abilities, is probably more positive than your perception of him. Therefore, it's likely that he won't be ready right away to jump in and join you in listing when and where he struggles. Furthermore, your child desperately wants to please you (even if he pretends that he doesn't care), so perceived criticism from you will make him feel pretty lousy and might trigger a defensive "So what?" kind of attitude.

So how do you tell your child that she has a problem with time management, without eliciting an eye roll and a claim that you are overreacting? How do you help your child recognize the mess that's in her backpack, without making her feel bad about it? Most important, how do you help her recognize that organizational skills may be areas of weakness for her, without making her feel criticized or attacked?

Because the program in this book depends on a partnership between you and your child, it's important to set a collaborative tone from the beginning. Consider these guidelines for starting with an open, honest conversation about your child's organizational strengths and weaknesses that is both positive and constructive.

Guide to the Glitches for Teens

It takes brains to do everything we do: breathing, eating, even sleeping. Of course, it takes brains to learn and go to school. Walking into the building, finding your class, saying "Hello" to your friends, reading, taking notes, and listening to your teachers all take brains. Our brains have different parts that help us complete different activities. For example, there are parts that help with reading, and other parts that help with math, or shooting baskets, or listening to music. There are also parts of the brain that help us stay organized. These parts help us look around and figure out what we have to do. We are going to call the parts that help us decide what to do and how to do it the Mastermind. The Mastermind helps us control our actions, making sure that we do important things.

The Mastermind is outstanding, but not perfect. Sometimes the Mastermind is not active enough. When you are tired or nervous or rushing around, the Mastermind does not work so well. And from work with kids, teenagers, and adults, we know that some people have trouble keeping the Mastermind active enough. Other people say that these kids and adults are careless or lazy. But we know that is **not true**. We know that people with problems getting and staying organized usually want to work hard and do well. They just have trouble keeping the Mastermind active enough.

We have learned that little, annoying problems develop when the Mastermind is not active enough. Your brain is more likely to make mistakes, and when that happens, we say that "Glitches" have gotten in the way. We like to think of Glitches as little creatures who live inside our brains and mess us up when we least expect it. Of course, what we're really talking about are tendencies that we all have to let down our guard and make mistakes that make us seem disorganized—but we've found that it's a little easier to think about these kinds of mistakes as mischievous creatures with specific tricks that we have to be on the lookout for. So here's the way we think about this: We all have Glitches creeping around in our brains. They get in the way by making us forget to use skills, like writing down our assignments or checking that we have the things we need before we leave the house. Have you ever forgotten a book or paper that you needed to take to school? If you have, that was the Glitches' work. Have you ever lost an important paper, like your homework or a special permission slip? That was also caused by Glitches. Every time we slip up and make mistakes—forgetting to hand in assignments, leaving important materials at school, taking too much time to finish homework, forgetting to plan ahead for a big project that is due—the Glitches are thrilled. They love it when we are not in control of our actions.

Let's find out who they are and what they do.

First, there is the **Go-Ahead-Forget-It Glitch.** This Glitch doesn't want you to

(continued)

remember important things, like homework assignments, important books that you need to bring home to study for a test, or the chore that you were asked to do. This Glitch *wants* you to forget things and get into trouble. When it wins, you look silly, and you will probably get into trouble with your parents or teachers.

There is also the **Go-Ahead-Lose-It Glitch.** This Glitch takes your mind off your things, so you misplace them or lose them. This Glitch tells you that you will find important papers no matter where you put them, so it convinces you just to stuff papers into your backpack or desk. When you can't find your things, the Go-Ahead-Lose-It Glitch has gotten you.

The **Time Bandit** is another Glitch. The Time Bandit makes you lose track of time and forget when things are due. The Time Bandit confuses you, so that you think things will take only a short time, or it distracts you while you're working, so that you don't use your time well.

Finally, the last Glitch, the **Go-Ahead-Don't-Plan Glitch,** takes away your good thinking skills. This Glitch tells you that you don't have to plan. It's thrilled when your projects or fun activities don't work out.

The Organizational Skills Training (OST) program was designed to help kids and teens learn how to use special skills to fight the Glitches. If you can learn and practice new ways to get organized, you can strengthen your Mastermind and keep the Glitches—and your life—under control.

Set the stage. Tell your child that you want to talk to him about some difficulties he's been having with staying organized, so that you can work together on these issues. Set a supportive tone by acknowledging that it may be hard to talk about problems, but that if the two of you are going to work together to make things go more smoothly, you need to start by figuring out what can be improved. Tell your child that you really want to hear about what's difficult for him in getting things done at home and school, and that you want to try to help him.

Consider your timing. Make sure you have the time and space to talk and won't be interrupted by ringing phones, nosy siblings (the last thing your child needs is a "peanut gallery" of siblings chiming in), or other demands. Also, consider your child's mood and physical state. Don't sit down to talk after she's come home from a full day of school and two after-school activities, when she's tired, or right before a meal. Think about what makes your child open up more in general. Does she talk more when you and your spouse are there, or would two of you in the room make her feel like she's being "ganged up on"? Does she open up more when you're sitting in your backyard, or does she need to be in a room with no distractions? Would a snack help her feel more relaxed?

Keep it brief. While you want to have a full discussion of organizational strengths and weaknesses with your child, you also need to be mindful of how long your child can sit and talk before he tunes out. Try to aim for an initial discussion of 5–10 minutes; if your child is engaged, you can keep talking. Keep in mind that this discussion is meant to be an overview, and that you will have the chance to delve more deeply into different skill areas later on.

Start with strengths. It's always a good idea to list strengths before moving on to discuss opportunities for improvement. Think about your child's organizational strengths, and praise specific actions that reflect good organization. For example, if your child keeps her Legos figures in perfect order or is always ready for swim practice with her bathing cap and suit, praise her for her organization in those areas. Explain that all of us (yourself included) have areas of strength and weakness when it comes to being organized.

Don't talk too much. If you find that you're doing all the talking, stop and ask a question, encouraging your child to mention what he's noticed about problems in different areas. If your child has nothing to contribute on a given topic (for instance, you ask about times when he doesn't plan ahead, and he can't think of anything), say something brief about what you've noticed in that domain and move on.

Don't judge. When you speak to your child about specific organizational issues that you have noticed, do so in a neutral, matter-of-fact way, without labeling these issues in negative terms. Also, be careful not to insert your own opinions about what your child "should" be doing. Stick to the facts without passing judgment. Finally, avoid blaming your child for her organizational weaknesses. Using the model of the "Glitches" will help you frame your comments in a nonblaming way.

Be supportive. Pay careful attention to your child's facial expressions and body language. Does he look upset or angry? Are his arms crossed defensively? Is he fidgeting or avoiding eye contact? If you notice any of these signs of discomfort, take a moment to check in and reset. Praise him for engaging in this conversation with you, and acknowledge how hard it can be for any of us to talk about things that aren't so easy for us to do.

🏆 ENHANCING SUCCESS

You might also want to suggest that the two of you do something special together after you're done with this discussion, to motivate your child to participate. It's always easier to sit through something boring or uncomfortable if you know that you get to make an ice cream sundae, play a round of video games, or go to the park afterward.

The following dialogue illustrates some sample interactions that might occur during such a discussion, with hints on ways of sensitively reviewing your child's thoughts and feelings. We call these types of exchanges throughout the book "Constructive Conversations."

💬 CONSTRUCTIVE CONVERSATIONS

Parent: I like this idea of Glitches that are out to get the Mastermind in trouble, because I feel like it describes really well how we can all run into problems when we aren't organized. What do you think? Did you recognize any of those Glitches' tricks?

Child: I guess so.

Parent: What about the Go-Ahead-Forget-It Glitch? I liked what it said about how that Glitch sometimes tricks you into thinking you'll remember everything, so you don't need to write it down . . . and then you forget something important.

Child: Well, sometimes I forget to write down one of my assignments, like my reading log. But I always remember everything I have to do anyway, so it doesn't really matter.

Parent: You're right. You do always remember to read, which is great! But can you think of a time when you forgot to write down an assignment, and then found out the next day that you didn't get a part of your homework done?

Child: Well, I guess that happens sometimes. Like last week, when I forgot to write down that I needed a book for my book report, and then I didn't have one when we needed to read in class.

Parent: That's a great example. You're doing a great job at being a part of this discussion. Let's think a little more about the other three Glitches, and then we can get some ice cream! Hmm . . . I know another Glitch that definitely lurks around this house—the Time Bandit.

Child: Ugh, I know what you're going to say.

Parent: What am I going to say?

Child: That I'm never ready on time, and I make you crazy every morning. You're always yelling at me about this!

Parent: I know, and I'm sorry about that. I hate starting my day yelling at you! But that's part of why we're talking about all of this: If we can figure out where the problems are, we can figure out better ways of dealing with them. Because I think we can agree that the way we're dealing with it now is not so great, huh? So what are the things that slow you down in the morning?"

Child: I'm always tired, so when I get out of bed, I move really slowly.

Parent: Ah, we were just reading about how the Time Bandit steals our time more when we're tired, right?

Child: Yeah, I guess that's true. And I just never think it will take that long to get ready, but it takes me time to pick my outfit and get dressed and eat breakfast and all that.

Parent: So this is definitely something we should work on together, because I feel stressed, you feel stressed, and that's not how we should start our day. I think it's great that you're thinking about all of this and recognizing what things we can work on and get better at.

Moving Forward

Once you have completed the OTMP Inventory and used it in briefly discussing problem areas with your child, you should have a better idea of how to focus your efforts as you move through the rest of this book and work with your child on improving organization.

Where to Start?

For most children, it makes sense to work through the chapters in Part III of this book in order, since the skills are presented from the simplest to the more complex; thus the later skills often depend on the earlier ones. For example, your child needs to have a good system in place for knowing what homework is assigned before he can work on managing time more effectively for homework. However, the OTMP Inventory can help you identify which Glitches are most problematic for your child (each chapter in Part III focuses on a particular Glitch) and which individual skills are most important for your child to build within a specific chapter (though we recommend reading through skills your child already seems to have, just in case you pick up some tips and tricks that could come in handy in the future). Taking stock of your child's organizational strengths and weaknesses can also help you manage both your and your child's expectations. It is likely that for problems your child experiences infrequently, she may acquire new skills fairly quickly, with guided practice; however, for more entrenched issues, you will need to apply more concerted effort and time.

As you review the items that are most problematic for your child on the OTMP Inventory, you may find that the issues with the biggest negative impact are all school-related. This isn't unusual (even if the impact carries over into a lot of conflict at home). In fact, as we've discussed in Chapter 1, the OST program was developed specifically to address the areas where children with organizational problems struggle, most of which relate to completion of school assignments and responsibilities. If this is the case for your child, you can just work through the Part III chapters in order, and then check Part IV to see if you want to work on problems that affect your child and you at home. Sometimes a weakness in a particular skill at school—say, packing the backpack—shows up similarly at home, as in packing sports bags or weekend bags for visits to relatives. In that case, it may be relatively easy to transfer the skills learned for backpack organization to organizing bags used at home. But sometimes children don't exhibit the same problems with a skill at home as they do at school. If your child's profile shows big problems with certain skills at home that are not problems at school (for instance, your child's room is a mess, but his school-related materials are in fairly good order), you may want to start working on those home problems at the same time as school problems. Chapter 11 will direct you to skill instructions you'll need from Part III, in addition to explaining how to apply them to a home issue. Reading through the whole book before starting on the program will provide a valuable overview.

Tracking Progress

You'll find tools for tracking your child's progress throughout the book, but you can also use the ratings on the OTMP Inventory for this purpose if you wish—especially to provide extra motivation to keep going. With extra copies of the Inventory on hand (again, see the end of the Contents for information on printing), you can choose a time interval at which to fill out the form again and see whether you can check off fewer boxes in the "Always" or "Often" columns . . . and celebrate your child's progress!

Chapter 4 will give you an overview of what to expect in Parts III and IV, where you'll be working on building the skills your child needs. You'll find essential tools for motivating your child to make changes in daily routines and maintain those changes over time in Chapter 5. These tools are built into every skills-building chapter in Parts III and IV, so be sure to read it thoroughly.

Understanding the Organizational Skills Training (OST) Program

Before moving on to Part II, where you'll lay the foundation for the skills-building work in Parts III and IV, have you . . .

- Gained an understanding of organizational skills and how they are related to the executive functions in your child's developing brain?
- Learned how the OST program was developed and how it can help children build important skills for success in school and at home?
- Gained an understanding of your role in helping your child reap the benefits of the OST program?
- Developed an understanding of your child's organizational skills and weaknesses?
- Gotten a preliminary idea of how you will work through this book, based on where your child needs the most help?

Part II

Laying
the Foundation
for Change

4

Overview of
the Skills-Building Program

In this chapter, you will learn how to:

- Pace yourself as you move through the steps in the Organizational Skills Training (OST) program.
- Navigate the chapters in Parts III and IV to help your child develop enhanced skills in tracking assignments, managing materials, managing time, and planning.

If you've followed the suggested steps outlined in Chapter 3, you should now have a better understanding of exactly how your child struggles with organization. At this point, you should have a grasp of specific skills that you want your child to learn. However, you may also be feeling a bit uneasy: You may be wondering how you are going to help your child learn these skills, which are so important for success in school and beyond. The task may seem daunting, especially if others (like teachers or tutors) have tried and failed to teach your child to keep books and papers in order, get things done on time, or plan ahead.

First of all, we want you to take a moment to recognize that you, as a parent, know your child better than anyone else. You also spend more time with your child than anyone else and have the ability to reach out to your child's teachers (the other people who spend the most time with your child) to enlist their support. Even when children who come to our clinic really want professional help for their organizational skills difficulties, we rely on parents to be the primary motivators of change. We teach each child and parent new routines, but without the parent's reminders, monitoring, and reinforcement between treatment sessions, we would never be able to motivate true change in the child's behavior.

In the chapters that follow, we'll share the tips and tricks that we have developed over the course of over a decade of research and rigorous evaluation on the OST program. We'll break down the components of this evidence-based clinical treatment and give you tools that can help your child become more organized. In addition to sharing our knowledge about the steps that kids can take to get more organized, we will teach you the best way to keep your child on track and motivated to beat the Glitches we described in Chapter 3.

The OST Program

In the clinical trial for OST, and in all of our clinical work with children and families, we have learned that parent involvement is key in helping children learn new organizational skills. In the clinical treatment, parents were involved in every session, so that they could prompt, monitor, praise, and reward their children for using new organizational skills/routines at home. We'll discuss in Chapter 5 how you can support your child's use of organization, time management, and planning (OTMP) skills, using the same procedures that worked in our research. Teacher involvement was also found to be important; in the clinical trial, teachers were asked to prompt, monitor, and praise the children's use of OTMP skills in the school setting. Chapter 6 will help you think about ways to involve your child's teacher in supporting OTMP skill use.

The OST treatment protocol is structured to follow a logical sequence—moving from basic organizational skills to more complex skills, and building the child's competence gradually within a supported framework. We have organized this book according to the same principles that proved effective in clinical trials of OST. We provide a suggested sequence of steps that you and your child can follow to build OTMP skills without overwhelming your child. Remember that if you want your child to work on an area that is challenging or downright unpleasant for him (like being more organized), you will need to make sure that your child has the chance to succeed. If you start out too quickly, expecting your child to conquer abstract organizational tasks (like planning) from the get-go, you will set him—and the program—up for failure. If, instead, you allow your child to master basic skills one at a time (like separating papers into categories and filing them), your child will be more willing and ready to try the next set of skills that you introduce.

This is why the OST program starts with simpler skills and then builds to more complex ones. It's also the reason we've cautioned in Chapter 3 against skipping ahead too quickly. Skipping over "smaller" steps (described in the earlier chapters in Part III) and moving directly to more complex skills can rob your child of the critical early experience of success and leave her without the fundamental skills needed to perform more complex organizational tasks.

The skills training portion of treatment begins with methods for tracking assignments, so that the child knows what to do each evening. Once a child is certain of the assignments, working on them requires having the needed papers, books, and other materials available. Therefore, skills for managing materials follow. Knowing the details of assignments and having the required materials are essential first steps in time management; after these skills are addressed, the child can focus on the other skills related to time management, including fitting tasks into a schedule and avoiding time-wasting distractions. All of the skills above are required for effective planning to occur, so task planning is introduced only after the child has learned how to track assignments, manage materials, and manage time.

In each chapter in Part III, we provide suggestions to help you determine when your child is ready to move on to the next skill, so that you can move through the program at a reasonable pace. Furthermore, in Chapter 5 we discuss other ways to support your child's mastery of new organizational routines, by prompting, monitoring, praising, and rewarding your child's positive behaviors.

Overview of Steps That Support Organization at School

Tracking Assignments

Chapter 7 focuses on tips and tricks that will help your child track school assignments. You will learn how to help your child use a simple but effective tool for recording daily assignments and noting materials needed for those assignments. In addition, you will learn how to support your child in keeping track of dates for upcoming tests and due dates for longer-term assignments on a calendar. These routines will help your child prepare better for the school-related tasks that must be completed on a daily basis and over longer periods of time. Knowing how to keep track of assignments is especially important once children reach middle school; students struggling with organization can easily lose track of what is due and when, leading to an avalanche of missed deadlines that increase feelings of stress and conflict with parents and teachers.

Managing Materials

Chapter 8 focuses on methods for organizing papers, books, and work areas. We provide strategies that will help your child practice a new way to organize and transfer papers, and use a simple checklist for effectively packing a backpack. We also present a suggested routine for getting work areas ready to go, so that all required materials are present and distracting items are put away. These routines related to managing materials will help children arrive at school and home with the materials they need and become more efficient in setting up work areas.

Time Management

Chapter 9 focuses on critical time management skills for daily homework completion. In this chapter we share tips that will help children learn to estimate how long it takes to complete tasks, and to determine when to fit tasks into their personal schedule. If your child struggles with telling time and calculating the passage of time, we also present guidelines and materials that can help you support these basic skills. In addition, we discuss how you can help your child develop strategies for controlling the Time Bandit, by identifying things that distract her and taking steps to manage those distractions. If you follow the steps outlined in this section, your child should be better able to estimate how much time should be dedicated to specific tasks and set up an after-school schedule that allows for appropriate work and fun time. We'll discuss how you can help support your child's use of time-planning skills by engaging in daily conferences and rewarding good time management skills.

Planning

Finally, in Chapter 10, we address planning—another area that is particularly important as children get older and must work on more long-term and multiple-step assignments. If you've ever had to stay up late with your child the night before a big project is due, printing out bibliographies or gluing last-minute touches onto science dioramas, you know exactly how important planning is. We'll help you understand the different components of good planning: breaking tasks down into their main steps, ordering the steps, getting needed materials, fitting the steps into the schedule so that the entire task is completed on time, and checking work for neatness and completeness. We discuss how you can prompt your child to use these different components through the use of a daily task-planning conference, and how to reinforce your child's planning for school assignments and projects.

Overview of Steps That Support Organization at Home

In Part IV of this book, we share tips and tricks that help children stay organized at home. School is not the only setting that demands organization. As children grow older, OTMP skills will help them become more independent at home. Sometimes it probably feels like you spend half your day nagging your child to put his things away, get ready on time, pack up his sports stuff, do chores without constant reminders, or plan ahead for activities or events. It doesn't have to be that way! With the right tools and guidance, your child *can* learn to keep track of his schedule, manage his things, complete daily tasks, and plan ahead, so that you don't have to do these tasks for him. Keep in mind that you'll need to refer to Part III for instructions in building specific skills for home organization, along with the tips in Part IV.

Moving Forward

So what will you be doing as you work your way through Parts III and IV? Details about the daily routine you'll be adopting are given in Chapter 5, but here is essentially what you can expect: You'll be listing goals on a behavior record and assigning points to your child for performing each behavior each day. These points will add up to earn the child rewards to keep her motivated. You'll also be keeping track of when the child has successfully performed each organizational task for a designated number of consecutive days, after which she will be considered to have mastered that skill, and you can move on to a new goal. To ensure that children succeed, we give practical tools and pointers throughout the book for prompting the desired behaviors, praising achievement, and rewarding progress.

5

Prompt, Monitor, Praise, Reward

How to Motivate Your Child Down the Path toward Organization

> In this chapter, you will learn how to:
> - Motivate your child to approach tasks at school and at home in a more organized way.
> - Use research-tested behavior management strategies to increase the chances that your child will consistently use organizational skills and routines.
> - Set a collaborative tone with your child.
> - Clarify your expectations.
> - Prompt your child to use specific skills.
> - Reinforce positive behaviors by praising and rewarding your child's actions.

Megan, a third grader, has been forgetting to bring her notebook and folder home from school a few nights each week, and her teacher has started to express concern about Megan's incomplete homework record. Megan's mother, deciding to take matters into her own hands, sits down with Megan one evening to talk to her about being more organized. Mom explains how important it is to keep track of books and folders for school, and suggests that Megan check her bag before leaving school every day, to make sure she has all the materials she needs to do her homework. She and Megan even come up with a great idea to help Megan remember to do this: They attach a bright pink key ring to the backpack zipper, which will cue Megan to check for her homework materials before leaving school. However, only two days after they have developed this plan, Megan comes home without her homework folder. Her mother is disappointed and frustrated; how could Megan forget something so simple? Why didn't the system work?

It's 7:00 P.M., and Derek is sitting on the couch, playing video games with his sister. He reports that he was done with his homework an hour ago. Derek's mom wanders into the study, where Derek had been doing his homework; she finds his completed math sheet on the desk, his planner on the chair, and his backpack on the floor, with the homework folder sticking out at an odd angle. She yells down the stairs to Derek, demanding that he come upstairs immediately and put his things away. Derek stomps up the stairs in annoyance, muttering under his breath about nagging moms.

If you've picked up this book, you have probably experienced something similar to these scenarios in your own home. While the content may vary, the theme remains the same: The child fails to carry out a small or large organizational task, and the parent often reacts with disappointment, frustration, and (after many small failures add up) anger. The child is angry and hurt by the parent's accusations, and, instead of feeling motivated to do better next time, may feel a sense of failure and hopelessness.

As discussed in Chapter 2, changing ingrained habits or behaviors is not easy for kids (or adults, for that matter). If you want your child to succeed in becoming more organized, you will need to go beyond telling him what to do differently; you will need to provide consistent support and guidance along the way.

 ENHANCING SUCCESS

Don't expect that simply telling your child what to do differently will magically change the way your child acts. Your child will need to practice new organizational skills repeatedly, with prompting and praise from you, before she can consistently use those skills.

Why It Helps to Prompt, Monitor, Praise, and Reward

When helping your child learn a new skill, you can maximize success by keeping in mind the four key steps introduced briefly in Chapter 2: **prompt, monitor, praise,** and **reward**. To learn a new behavior, your child needs to learn when to perform the new behavior and exactly what steps to follow. You can help with this by providing clear *prompts* at appropriate times. You can also help your child by closely *monitoring* performance of the new behavior, and by providing *praise* and *rewards* when your child demonstrates the new behavior. When you praise a positive behavior, it is likely that your child will perform that behavior again in the future (hoping to get another thumbs-up from you). Furthermore, when you provide a concrete reward, your child will remember the positive consequences of using that behavior and will be more likely to incorporate the behavior into his regular routines.

Setting the Ground Rules

One of the most important lessons you've undoubtedly learned from parenting is that children crave structure. This applies to learning organizational skills as well as to all other aspects of childrearing. For daily tasks and routines, it will help tremendously if you have clearly laid out the expected steps, rules, and actions ahead of time. We generally recommend that for set routines (homework completion, getting ready in the morning, bedtime rituals, etc.), parents lay out specific rules and guidelines for behavior—and write those expectations out, so that children can refer to them regularly.

Having **concrete, written rules** helps reduce the need to nag children to complete regular tasks. It also reduces arguments about why a reward has not been given for rules not followed: You can simply point to the rule in question. If Derek's mom had developed a list of homework rules that included a final step, "Put your homework materials back in your backpack," she could have simply referred Derek to the posted rules instead of nagging him to complete the last step.

For a child who struggles with organization, it is especially important to display a written list of homework rules. Work with your child to develop these rules to give her a sense of ownership over them, and invite your child to help illustrate or decorate them, or to print the rules in fancy fonts. Of course, you have the final say in determining what rules go on the list. But we've found that children are surprisingly tough on themselves when asked what rules would be most effective for them. We've provided a sample dialogue that can help you guide the conversation when creating homework rules with an elementary- or middle-school-age child, but first it's wise to consider how you would like homework to be done:

1. **When?** If your child's schedule varies on different days of the week, you can either try to create one rule that applies to every night or set up different nightly schedules. Don't forget to specify when any weekend homework should be completed (for instance, Saturday morning or Sunday afternoon).

2. **Where?** The best place to do homework really depends on your child and household. Some children work better when they are sprawled out comfortably on a couch; others work better at a desk. Some work better with a little noise around them (like at a kitchen table), and others work better in total silence (so they might be better off in their own rooms). A location relatively free of distractions is usually best, and obviously it should contain the basic materials your child will need to get homework done—computer, paper, pencils, markers, and so on.

3. **What else can your child do?** Be as specific as possible. Consider activities such as playing music (some children work better when music is playing; others do not), watching TV, texting, e-mailing, checking social media accounts, surfing the Internet, playing with toys, and talking with siblings.

4. **What if your child has a question?** Are you OK with your child's asking questions as she moves through her work, or would you prefer that she complete the assignments she can do independently first and save questions for the end? Or would you like to check in at specified intervals (such as every 15 minutes) and answer questions at those time points only? Is your child allowed to contact a friend to ask for help? Again, the rule that you specify should make sense for you: It should take into account other demands on your time, your child's work style (some children are incapable of moving on if they feel "stuck," while others are more comfortable going on), and your child's age and intellectual abilities.

5. **When should homework be finished?** Think about how long your child's homework generally takes, as well as your nightly routine. Clearly state what time you expect your child to be done with homework each evening (for instance, "Homework is completed by 7:00 P.M."). If you don't have

a good sense of how long your child should be spending on homework, we provide tips and tools in Chapter 9 for helping your child estimate how long work should take. You want to make sure that your rule is as specific as possible; therefore, if homework should take an hour each night, but might take additional time if there is a test or a major report due the next day, spell that out in the rules.

6. **What else?** Do you want to add a rule that all homework materials must be returned to the backpack after all assignments are done? Or a rule that a parent (or other adult) must check all work?

Homework rules should clearly lay out all of your expectations, so that your child knows exactly what to do to complete this routine successfully.

CONSTRUCTIVE CONVERSATIONS

Parent: You know how you have "class rules" at school that the teacher sets with you on the first day? I think it would be really helpful for us to have a list of homework rules, so that it's really clear what needs to be done— and how—when you do your work at home.

Child: Why do we need homework rules? I know what to do—get my homework done! It's pretty simple.

Parent: Yes, of course that's the goal. You should have your homework done by the end of the evening. But sometimes we end up arguing about the steps you're supposed to take to get to that goal—like whether you can check your texts while you're working, how many breaks you can take, what to do when you're having trouble with a particular math problem, and stuff like that. If we set up some rules that we can both follow, it might help make homework time go more smoothly.

Child: I guess so . . .

Parent: So let's think about what makes sense. First, let's talk about timing. What time do you think it makes sense to start homework each night?

Child: Well, it depends. When I have swim team right after school, I get home at 5:30 and can't start until about 6, after I eat dinner.

Parent: Right, but on other nights, you can start earlier. I know you like to unwind after you get home for about half an hour, and that makes sense. So why don't we say you'll start homework half an hour after you get home—that would be about 4:00 on a regular night, and about 6:00 on a swim team night. Now, where should we say you must do your home-work?

Child: Well, I've been sort of doing it wherever I want, but I sometimes have a harder time concentrating when I work at the kitchen table and other people are walking in and out of the kitchen.

Parent: Great point! You do have a desk in your room. Should we try out a new rule, and see if you can get your work done there every night?

Child: OK. But all the pens and markers and glue and stuff are downstairs, so it's not so easy for me to work at my desk.

Parent: That's a really good point. I'll buy an extra set of everything and work with you to set up your desk so that you can get your work done there. But if you're working in your room, we should probably also set a rule about what else you can or cannot be doing while you work—because with all your toys and things around you, it might be tempting to do other stuff while you're working.

Child: OK, so how about if we say, "No playing with other stuff while doing homework," or something like that?

Parent: That's perfect. So if I come in to check on you and see you working on your Legos, I can remind you of that rule.

It can be complicated to come up with homework rules that work well for your family and cover all eventualities. Typically, when working with families, we help them draft a set of rules, have them try these out for a week or so, and then help them rewrite as needed, to make sure that the rules are all-inclusive and appropriate. You will probably find that revising the rules is necessary; changes are fine, as long as you clearly discuss them with your child and rewrite the rules accordingly. Finally, remember that there are no "right" or "wrong" rules. As long as your rules are clear, specific, and reflective of your family's expectations, they will serve as effective guides for positive behavior.

Positive Prompts

Using this book, you will teach your child how to use organizational skills in specific situations where those skills are needed. For example, you might ask your child to check her backpack before school for items she needs that day. However, no child is likely to hear this instruction and suddenly begin performing this check every day from now on. You'll need to prompt your child, especially for the first few weeks after she learns the new skill, to perform this action. How does this work? It's quite simple:

1. **Move close to your child.** Don't yell a prompt across the room; your child is more likely to ignore you, making this a wasted reminder.

2. **Get your child's attention.** For instance, make eye contact.

3. **Ask for one thing at a time.** If you give your child multiple reminders at once, odds are that she will forget at least one of them.

4. **Be clear:** "Please put your folders in your bag" (vs. "Pack up").

5. **Use a positive, encouraging voice.** Even though you may be understandably frustrated by your child's difficulty with following through on organizational tasks, try your best to keep that frustration out of your voice when you deliver a prompt.

6. **Don't nag!** When you nag your child, especially about something you've nagged him about before, it is quite likely that what your child hears after the fifth or sixth time is "Blah, blah, blah" or "Mom/Dad's just griping again."

7. **Stick with the present; forget about the past:** "Please pack your bag with your homework materials" (vs. "Let's see if you can actually remember to pack up your stuff today, unlike yesterday").

As your child becomes more comfortable with a specific organizational task, fewer prompts will be needed. But don't taper them off until you notice a change in your child's behavior. If you've been giving daily prompts to pack the backpack, you can probably decrease your prompts once you notice your child automatically going through the process of checking that everything is in the backpack. It may take a couple of weeks, but at that point you might prompt only every other night, then cut down to every three nights, then once a week, and finally stop prompting altogether—assuming that as you step back your prompts, your child continues to use the skill consistently.

 Tip for Older Children

Prompting can become especially complicated as your child approaches middle school and beyond. As children get older, they often hear prompts as nagging, regardless of how hard you try to be neutral and positive. One way to manage this is to discuss with your older child how he would like to be prompted. First, explain why prompting is important: Let your child know that when you prompt him to do something, you're not trying to nag or criticize him, but would like to provide a helpful reminder. You may want to share how reminders help you when you're learning a new task (e.g., a reminder from a friend to pick up your child's carpool on a day when you don't ordinarily do so). Then ask your child how you can provide that kind of reminder for organizational tasks in a way that's most helpful and least intrusive. Would your child prefer that you write down or e-mail reminders, instead of providing them out loud? Can you use specific words each time (e.g., "Assignment list check!" or "Plan ahead!"), so that your child knows what to expect and is not thrown off by your language? Who would be the best person to deliver prompts—you, your babysitter, or your child's other parent/your partner? As long as the system works for you and your child, there is no "right" or "wrong" way to set up prompts. Your older child might also be able to tell you when he has mastered the new routine, so that you know when to fade out prompts for that task.

 CONSTRUCTIVE CONVERSATIONS

Here are some examples of "good" prompts:

"Please put your books in your backpack."

"It's time to start your homework. Please get your desk ready by clearing off the extra materials."

"Let's think about the schedule for today. How long do you think it will take to finish your homework?"

"Let's look at the clock. You have 15 minutes before we have to leave for soccer. I want you to get the rest of the math problems on this sheet done before we leave."

"Remember to follow all the homework rules on the list."

"Look at Rule 6: No music during homework time."

Masterful Monitoring: The Home Behavior Record

Use a chart to call attention to behaviors. Keeping track of when and how often your child uses a skill is key to motivating your child to keep up the good work. We've found it's best to use a written chart, which can be displayed in a prominent place in your home (for instance, on the refrig-erator door, on a bulletin board, or above your child's desk). In our work with families and children, we've found that a chart forces both parents and children to pay more attention to the behavior in question, and thus is an important first step in motivating change in that behavior. Sometimes it's hard to notice when your child moves from writing down homework two days in one week to three days in the next week to four days in the following week. The days the homework is missed are the ones that usually stand out. Tracking helps everyone become more mindful of slow, steady improvements.

We have created a chart, the Home Behavior Record or HBR (see page 59), to help you monitor your child's use of the organizational skills and routines that you will introduce as you work through the chapters in Parts III and IV. Once you've prompted your child in a clear, specific, and positive way, you will monitor whether or not your child follows through on practicing the goal by recording the child's skill use on the HBR. Using this chart on a daily basis will be your single most important job in helping your child through this program. Each week you should create a new HBR for your child, with five target goals listed (such as "Has all assignments written down in planner," "No loose papers in backpack," and three others). You should set aside a few minutes each day to sit down with your child and award the points she has earned. (See the end of the Contents for informa-tion on printing extra copies of the HBR, or accessing an enlarged version that allows more space for adding new goals.)

In Chapter 7, the first chapter of Part III, you'll be given five goals to use on your first HBR. At the end of the week, take a look to see how your child has done with each goal. At the end of each chapter in Part III, we'll give you a list of "mastery criteria"—concrete targets indicating that your child has truly learned and ingrained a given skill, and is ready to move that goal off the HBR and add a new one in its place. If your child has mastered any goals, give him a big cheer and begin to teach him the next skill explained in Part III. Take the mastered goal off the new week's HBR, and replace it with the goal listed for the new skill you've taught. As you'll see in Chapter 7, many goals take two weeks to master, so don't be surprised if your child's HBR for Week 2 looks largely the same as the record for Week 1.

As you move through each chapter in Parts III and IV, we will cue you to add specific behaviors to the HBR as you introduce new skills to your child. Once your child is earning points for a specific goal very consistently (meeting the mastery criteria in Part III), she can "graduate" from that goal. You can remove each mastered skill from the HBR and begin working on

Home Behavior Record (HBR)
Goals to Prompt, Monitor, Praise, and Reward

Give your child 1 point for each goal that is performed on a given day. There are 5 possible points to be earned each day.

Behaviors	Day 1	Day 2	Day 3	Day 4	Day 5	Day 6	Day 7
Goal 1:							
Goal 2:							
Goal 3:							
Goal 4:							
Goal 5:							
Total points (out of 5):							
Total points for the week:							

a new skill, adding the suggested new goal to the empty spot on the HBR. In this way, we will walk you through a learning program that will help you not only teach your child new skills, but also motivate your child's success by following through with appropriate monitoring.

Powerful Praise

It may not always seem like it, but your attention and approval are very important to your child. Your child will work hard to get your positive attention and will repeat behaviors that you praise, especially if you use praise in a targeted way.

Use labeled praise. When your child does something positive, use "labeled praise" to let him know exactly what he did well. For example, instead of telling your child, "You've been doing a good job recently," tell him, "You've been ready for school every day this week. Great job!" Using labeled praise during an activity helps your child stay focused on what is important and learn what steps to repeat in the future. The pointers in the box on below will guide you in using labeled praise.

Find your praise style. Praising in a sincere, specific, and enthusiastic manner will increase your child's motivation to continue acting in a positive way. You don't have to be sugary-sweet or fake; just use your own style

---

Pointers to Keep Your Child on Track with Labeled Praise

- Provide labeled praise often, especially when your child is learning a new behavior.
- Notice and praise small behaviors that lead to a goal—for example, "You put back each homework sheet as soon as you were done with it. What a great idea to make sure you get all your homework back in your folder!"
- Use your own style. You don't have to be a cheerleader. Show some excitement, but don't act like a completely different person.
- Sometimes a simple "Thank you" is helpful.
- *Do not* pay attention to small misbehaviors in the middle of praising your child.

and your own words to praise your child and to indicate what you like about what the child has done. As long as you are honest and positive in pointing out what you like about your child's behavior, your praise will be effective.

Pay attention to your child's response. Some children are uncomfortable with praise. If that is the case for your child, you can simply point out what your child did that was positive, and thank her or indicate that you are giving her a point on the HBR: For example, "You wrote down all the assignments for tonight in your planner! Let's put a point down on the HBR."

 Tip for Older Children

Preteens and teenagers, in particular, are notorious for eye rolls in the face of parents' praise—but more often than not, they actually appreciate it.

 ENHANCING SUCCESS

If you are unsure about how your child will react to praise, try this experiment: Offer your child some genuine praise, but don't pay attention to how she responds to you verbally. Instead, notice if she repeats the behavior you praised over the next week or so. If she does, it's likely that your words made a difference.

 CONSTRUCTIVE CONVERSATIONS

Labeled praise might sound like this:

"Good job! You checked to make sure all of your papers were put in your folder."

"Great, you cleared your desk for homework."

"Wow! You have all of your things in your bag."

"Nice job. Your homework supplies are all out and ready."

"This is wonderful; you have all of your homework listed on your assignment sheet."

"Thank you; you helped by putting your toys back in the storage bin."

Reinforcing with Rewards

Praise is valuable, but providing small, appropriate rewards when children use those skills can encourage consistent use of new skills. Because children are concrete thinkers, rewards provide valuable, "hands-on" reinforcement that helps them recognize the link between specific behaviors and positive consequences. Your child may or may not be motivated to keep a neat desk or get good grades in school—but he will probably be motivated to earn extra screen time after completing homework. Don't worry that you are "bribing" the child. Even if your child is writing down assignments only to earn a reward (and not because he has magically bought into the notion that organization is a valuable life skill), the end result will be the same: Your child will learn how to manage daily tasks in a more organized way.

Creating a Points-and-Rewards System

In the OST program, we guide parents in the construction of a points-and-rewards system linked to the HBR, which allows for the consistent, appropriate use of rewards. The system is quite simple, and we have found that it works well: The child earns points each day for successful use of the organized behaviors listed on the HBR, and the parent provides rewards based on the number of points earned. The reward system is based on standard behavior management methods, which have been proven to be effective in motivating behavior change. You may have tried similar methods with your child and found that they do not work or that they seem to wane in effectiveness over time. We provide "Enhancing Success" ideas that will help you develop a system that has the best chance of working for you, along with "Troubleshooting Tips" to address common challenges.

Daily and weekly rewards. Consider providing a small reward at the end of each day and a larger reward at the end of each week, for cumulative use of the skills. Daily rewards keep a child interested in performing specific behaviors each day; this is especially important for young children, who respond best to immediate rewards. Weekly rewards help children stay interested in using the behaviors over time and teach them about the advantages of consistent effort.

The structure of this rewards system can be particularly helpful for kids who struggle with organizational skills. Children who have difficulties with executive functioning often have brains that are hard-wired to respond better to short-term rewards than long-term rewards. Since good grades are long-term rewards, they are often less motivating for these kids. This reward system restructures things so that a child is working to achieve a small goal that will result in a concrete reward the same day, rather than a large goal that will yield an intangible reward at the end of the marking period.

🏆 ENHANCING SUCCESS

If your family's schedule is very tight and will not allow for daily rewards, be sure to award *points* (with praise) every day on the HBR, and consistently provide a weekly reward that is motivating to the child (see below for more on identifying appropriate rewards).

Points system. The HBR usually has five target goals for the child to perform, so the child can earn up to 5 points each day. You will select the target goals based on the skills you are working on with your child at a particular time. In each chapter in Part III, we'll guide you with suggestions for specific goals to add to the HBR as you move through the program. You want to be able to reward the child each day for good performance (i.e., 3 out of 5 points), and also to provide an extra-special reward for excellent performance (e.g., at least 4 out of 5 points).

Daily and weekly reward menus. On the following page you'll find a sample daily reward menu that gives examples of Level One and Level Two rewards, which are awarded for good and excellent performance, respectively. For weekly rewards, you should also identify two levels on your reward menu; Level One is selected when the child earns 60% (15 out of 25 points) of the points available over the course of the week, and Level Two is selected if the child earns at least 80% (20 out of 25) of the points available over the course of the week. See page 64 for a sample weekly reward menu.

🔍 Troubleshooting Tip

You'll find that on some days there are target goals on the HBR that are not applicable (e.g., following the homework rules on a day when no homework is assigned). In these cases, award a Level One prize if 60% of the possible points are earned (without the task that's not applicable for this day), and a Level Two prize if at least 80% of the possible points are earned. The same goes for weekly rewards.

Sample Daily Reward Menu

LEVEL ONE REWARDS

    15 minutes of music/video game time
    15 minutes of playing ball outside
    15 minutes of playing on computer/tablet

LEVEL TWO REWARDS

    30 minutes of music/video game time
    30 minutes of playing ball outside
    30 minutes of playing on computer/tablet

For an HBR with five target goals:

    Level One: Use if the child earns 60% (3 out of 5) of the points for the
        day.
    Level Two: Use if the child earns at least 80% (4 out of 5) of the points
        for the day.

Sample Weekly Reward Menu

LEVEL ONE REWARDS

    Download a movie
    Breakfast at favorite restaurant
    Bike ride in the park with Dad
    $2 to buy music or apps

LEVEL TWO REWARDS

    See a movie in a theater
    Visit the zoo
    Go bowling
    $5 in digital music/game credits

For an HBR with five target goals:

    Level One: Use if the child earns 60% (15 out of 25, if you're counting week-
        days only) of the points accumulated over the course of the week.
    Level Two: Use if the child earns at least 80% (20 out of 25, weekdays
        only) of the points accumulated over the course of the week.

Assigning points carefully. Be kind and generous with your words and encouragement, but very strict in awarding points and rewards. Make sure you give rewards only when your child has legitimately and completely earned them; do not allow your child to renegotiate the limits of your agreement. (Many children are excellent lawyers-in-training!) Leaving any gray area (for example, awarding points when your child swears that she wrote down her assignments, but she left the assignment record at school) will encourage your child to argue about whether a reward should be given, and test to see what wiggle room she can have while still earning a reward.

Identifying appropriate rewards. The rewards must be motivating for *your child*, and every child has different interests, so be sure to involve your child in the creation of the reward menus. You may need to rotate or change items on a reward menu after a few weeks if your child seems to be less motivated to earn points or has clearly changed interests. On the following pages you'll find a form with questions you can use to guide a discussion with your child about what rewards would be most enticing, and to sort rewards into highly (Level Two) and moderately (Level One) valuable categories. (See the end of the Contents for information on printing this form, so you can revise your child's reward menus as needed.)

 Troubleshooting Tip

Are you concerned about what rewards might cost? Some parents worry that giving rewards regularly will end up being costly. Rewards for reinforcing organized behavior should not cost you a lot of money. In fact, activities/privileges are often more rewarding to children than items that cost money.

Suggestions for Selecting Rewards

The following are some suggestions that have helped us work with parents to select appropriate rewards.

1. Are there privileges that your child currently gets "for free" that could be reconsidered and restricted? For example, many children use electronic devices (computer, iPad, tablet, smartphone, Wii, Xbox, TV, etc.) each day and highly value their time spent on those devices. You might be able to change the rules regarding use of electronic devices slightly, so that your child can earn extra time on the devices, based on the number of

Questions for Developing a Reward Menu

1. What does your child like to do during free time?

Activity	How often does your child engage in this activity?	Does your child get to engage in this activity for free (that is, without needing to "earn" the privilege)?	Rate how highly the child values this activity (1 = very low value; 5 = very high value)

2. What toys or other items does your child like to use?

Toy or other item	How often does your child use this toy/item?	Does your child get to use this toy/item for free?	Rate how highly the child values this toy/item (1 → 5)

3. What outings does your child enjoy?

Outing	How often does your child go on this outing?	Does your child get to go on this outing for free?	Rate how highly the child values this outing (1 → 5)

(continued)

4. With whom does your child like to play?

Person	How often does your child play with this person?	Does your child get to play with this person for free?	Rate how highly the child values playing with this person (1 → 5)

5. Does your child collect any items or show interest in collecting items?

Item	How often does your child collect this item?	Does your child get to collect this item for free?	Rate how highly the child values this item (1 → 5)

6. Does your child have any favorite snacks or restaurants?

Food or restaurant	How often does your child eat this food or go to this restaurant?	Does your child get to have this type of food or eat at this restaurant for free?	Rate how highly the child values this food or restaurant (1 → 5)

7. What does your child like to do on weekends (for example, play with a neighbor, have a sleepover with a friend)?

Activity/outing	How often does your child engage in this activity?	Does your child get to engage in this activity for free?	Rate how highly the child values this activity (1 → 5)

points earned on the HBR. The way you structure those rules will depend on what works for your family. Some parents find that their children need to unwind for half an hour or so right after school with a TV show or game before starting homework. For those parents, it might make sense to make that first TV show or game session "free" and then require that the child earn a minimum level of points on the HBR to get additional time with TV or other electronic devices. Other parents might decide that all time on electronic devices must be earned. There is no right or wrong decision in this regard; just make sure that you consider what will realistically work for your family before you set up the reward system.

2. If you decide to use time on electronic devices as a reward, Level One and Level Two rewards can be defined in terms of incremental amounts of time on the selected device (e.g., 15 minutes on a tablet as a Level One reward and 30 minutes as a Level Two reward). Another idea that can work well, if your child really wants a special electronic device or other toy (like a new video game) and the cost is reasonable, is to buy the device/toy and put it in a "library." Your child can then check the item out for a specified amount of time after earning a certain amount of points.

3. For older children, the opportunity to earn small amounts of money may be very rewarding if they enjoy saving up cash for their own purchases. Alternatively, you could deposit money into an online account, based on the number of points earned.

 Troubleshooting Tip

Is your reward system sustainable? Make sure you set up a reward system that you can carry out *consistently*. If you promise your child a reward and then cannot follow through, you will lose legitimacy, and your child will be less likely to buy into the system.

If you have answered the questions for developing a reward menu and are still having trouble thinking of possible rewards, these ideas have worked for parents in our program:

Daily Rewards

Special time with parent (reading, puzzles, games, time outdoors, etc.)
Electronic device time (child can earn less time for fewer points and more time for more points)

Art/drawing materials

Staying up 15–30 minutes past bedtime (depending on the number of points earned)

Choosing dinner/dessert

Time for riding bike/playing outside

Getting out of doing a chore

Weekly Rewards

Dinner or lunch at a restaurant

Trip to the park/zoo/bowling alley/movies/other special destination

Renting a movie

Having a friend over for a sleepover

Getting out of doing a chore

Small toys/collectibles

Credit for electronic apps or games or digital music

Trip to the dollar store

Managing Rewards

As mentioned above, the way you use the points-and-rewards system will determine how successful it is in motivating improved behavior. There are a few important tips to keep in mind as you manage the system for your child.

1. Deliver rewards with labeled praise. Your child should know exactly why she has earned the specified reward. As you award points on the HBR for each skill that your child has used, praise her for each action. Then tell your child that she can choose a reward from the reward menu because of her good/excellent performance.

2. Don't mix good news with bad. When you give rewards for using the organized behaviors on the HBR, don't bring up any negative things the child may have done that day. If your child was fighting with his sibling, you may need to give a separate consequence for that behavior; however, you should *not* take away the reward that the child has earned for the HBR tasks (writing down assignments, packing the backpack, completing homework on time, etc.) The rewards that are linked to the HBR should be kept separate from other rewards or punishments that you may use for other behaviors.

3. Be consistent, and model organized behavior. It is not simple to manage a reward system—especially as a busy parent with multiple demands on

your time. If you commit to rewarding your child for using new organizational skills, you must follow through with your end of the bargain; otherwise, your child will lose faith in the system and will not be motivated to try using the new organized behaviors. Therefore, think carefully about what steps you can follow to make points and rewards part of your new routine. For instance, figure out where to put the HBR so that you don't forget to award points; post the daily and weekly reward menus somewhere visible, so that you and your child are reminded of the consequences of positive behavior; and/or set a reminder on your phone to give a nightly reward.

> Remember, to maximize success for your child:
> Prompt
> Monitor
> Praise
> Reward

Pulling It All Together

After reading this chapter, you may wonder how you are going to remember to implement all of these principles as you try to support your child's organized behavior. Don't worry; we have built our own prompts into the next sections of the book, which will help you figure out when to add behaviors to the HBR and how to brainstorm issues that might come up with points and rewards along the way. As long as you remember to *prompt, monitor, praise, and reward* as your child learns new organizational skills and routines, you will be taking a huge step in helping your child succeed. Let's review how these four steps work together, with an example:

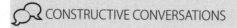 CONSTRUCTIVE CONVERSATIONS

Prompt–Monitor–Praise–Reward (P-M-P-R)

Prompt: "Grace, please check your backpack to make sure you have everything you need for school tomorrow."

Monitor: "You used your backpack checklist to check that your books and papers were all in your backpack. You get 1 point on the HBR!" (Write a "1" next to "Used backpack checklist" on the HBR.)

Praise: "Excellent job; you remembered to use your backpack checklist to make sure you have what you need!"

Reward: "You now have 5 points on the HBR for today. Great job! You get to choose a reward from Level Two on the reward menu."

Moving Forward

The strategies in this chapter give you the basic formula for helping your child make real and lasting changes. You are now ready to start using these tools to help your child take the first steps in becoming organized. The chapters in Part III provide specific strategies, tips, and tricks that will help you take your child step by step down the path to organization. First, however, Chapter 6 offers suggestions for making connections with your child's school to carry out the OST program.

6

Building a Connection between Home and School

In this chapter, you will learn how to:

- Identify a "point person" at your child's school (your child's teacher or a support staff member) who can help support your child's use of organizational skills.
- Conduct an initial meeting with this person.

Identifying a Single "Point Person" at the School

If you want your child to integrate new organizational skills and routines into his everyday life, you will need to enlist support and involvement from teachers and other key support staff at his school. It's helpful to identify a single "point person" at the school with whom you can communicate while working on this program. The appropriate person to fill this role differs, depending on the school context. In elementary school, more often than not, it is simplest to work directly with the child's classroom teacher. Beyond elementary school, when a child has many teachers, the situation is usually more complicated. It's often useful to start at the top (with the principal or headmaster), explain the type of help you need (by the end of this chapter, you'll have a good sense of the assistance required), and ask for advice regarding who might be the most useful partner in this endeavor. Possible contacts include a school psychologist, guidance counselor, or advisor; a staff member from student support services; the lead teacher of a teaching team; or a learning specialist.

If the child is assigned a paraprofessional (a teaching assistant whose role is to provide additional instructional and/or behavioral support) or aide, this can be a useful person to bring into the fold as you work on this program. Be clear about the skills that you plan to help your child develop, and describe exactly how you would like the paraprofessional to help. Explain that you would like to work together to find ways that the paraprofessional can support your child in learning those skills. In particular, you can request that the person prompt and praise your child, rather than doing tasks for the child. For example, you may ask the paraprofessional to prompt your child to write the assignments on the planner, and then initial these to indicate that they were recorded correctly, rather than writing down the assignments for your child.

Why Teachers/School Personnel Are Essential

Understanding and Support

First, it's important for teachers and other involved staff members to understand the challenges your child is facing and your plan for addressing them. The key issues you want them to understand are that your child struggles to learn organizational skills that are easier for many kids to develop (in other words, she is not just lazy), and that you are working with her on developing these skills in a step-by-step fashion. A teacher who understands that a child is working on writing down assignments and will get to time management later is more likely to notice positive changes in assignment tracking, rather than just focusing on a late assignment. The teacher will also be more likely to praise positive steps that the child takes toward getting organized, as opposed to criticizing failures to meet larger organizational demands.

Prompts at School

Second, as we've discussed in Chapter 5, your child will require frequent prompting when he is first learning a new organizational skill, before that skill becomes part of an established routine. We've found that children are more likely to master skills when teachers and other staffers know which new skills children are working on and prompt them to perform those skills at appropriate times. For example, the first new skill that we introduce to children is the use of a Daily Assignment Record (DAR), where the child must write down assignments, materials needed, and due dates. (The DAR is described in full in Chapter 7.)

Third grader Juan had a teacher who was excited about the OST program and enthusiastic about the value of the DAR. Each day she prompted Juan to turn to a blank DAR page and write down the assignments and materials needed. She then reviewed the list for accuracy, and she gave Juan a check mark on his DAR if he had recorded everything correctly. Juan quickly learned to use the DAR correctly; he was also proud that he was able to earn points at home for the positive feedback received from his teacher.

In contrast, fourth grader Rebecca consistently came home with partially completed or blank DARs. She was disappointed that she was unable to earn all of her daily points, because her teacher rarely remembered to review or sign her DAR. Rebecca often forgot to fill out the DAR on her own, and even when she remembered, she was shy about going up to the teacher's desk and asking for a check mark. It took several months for Rebecca to learn to use the DAR consistently, and she continued to forget materials at school as a result.

To set your child up for success, it's important to ensure that responsible adults can provide reminders and praise at the time when the skill is needed—especially when your child is just learning to use new, unfamiliar skills or routines.

Approval for Organizational Tools

Another reason why teachers/school staffers are vital members of the organizational "team" is that they often need to give approval for new organizational tools or systems.

Roger, a sixth grader who struggled with paper management, illustrates how essential this approval can be. Roger often forgot to punch holes in his papers to store them properly in the recommended three-ring binders, and his papers would get shoved into the front pocket of the binder or would be left to float in the bottom of the backpack. After working with an OST therapist, Roger started using an accordion file, which made it much easier for him to file papers correctly. However, a few days after he started using the accordion file, Roger was sent home with a note saying that he needed to use the same system for storing papers as the rest of the students. Because his parents had not cleared this new system with the teacher ahead of time, Roger was given negative feedback for his efforts to organize himself and was back at square one.

We've found that teachers vary widely in how explicitly they teach organizational skills or require the use of specific tools/systems. It's important to approach teachers and other school staff members at the outset and work together to figure out which systems work best for your child and which modifications may be acceptable. In all of Part III (Chapters 7–10), we suggest alternatives to the specific tools and routines that we recommend, with the understanding that some flexibility may be necessary to accommodate the specific demands of the child's school environment. We believe you'll find—as we have found—that when parents work hand in hand with teachers, changes to children's organizational routines are most lasting and beneficial.

How to Get Teachers/Other Staff Involved

To set the stage for a coordinated effort that will enhance your child's organized behavior in school, schedule an initial meeting with the teacher and/ or other identified "point person." (From here on, we'll refer to this person simply as "the teacher," for simplicity's sake.) At this meeting, you will:

1. Learn more from the teacher about your child's organizational performance in class.

2. Determine what organizational routines/tools the teacher asks the students to use, and how those are working for your child.

3. Determine whether the teacher is willing to work with you to prompt, monitor, and praise your child's use of new organizational routines/tools.

To accomplish the first goal, you will want to make sure that you focus the meeting on specific questions about your child's organizational strengths and weaknesses in school. To guide this conversation, you can refer to the behaviors listed on the Teacher's Organization, Time Management, and Planning (OTMP) Inventory (page 77). (See the end of the Contents for information on downloading and printing additional copies of this form.) You may want to ask the teacher to fill out this inventory before your meeting, so you can then discuss problems that the teacher notes as frequently affecting your child's performance in school.

To accomplish the second goal, finding out what steps the teacher has already taken to improve your child's organization in school, you can use the questions in the Teacher Interview form on page 78. (See the end of the Contents for information on downloading and printing extra copies of the form.)

You and the teacher may disagree about your child's problems with organization. In fact, children often act differently in different settings. For example, some children are moderately organized at school, where organizational routines are built into the schedule, but struggle to get homework done at home, where routines are less structured. Other children might manage organizational demands at home quite well, with one-on-one support from a parent, but fail to keep track of materials or get work done on time in class, without that individualized support. Your goal in this initial meeting is to understand how the teacher perceives your child's organizational strengths and weaknesses in school, as you want to work together to devise strategies to improve performance in that setting.

Your third task is to enlist the teacher's active participation in working with you and your child on an organizational program. You may want to share portions of this book with the teacher, including either the child or teen version of the Guide to the Glitches (see Chapter 3), which helps to explain how you will be discussing and approaching organizational difficulties with your child. You may also want to let the teacher know that the principles and techniques you will be using from this book were developed in an intervention called the Organizational Skills Training (OST) program, which has been shown to be effective in research studies.

Explain that you will be working with your child at home on learning key organizational skills and integrating those new skills into a regular routine. You can share portions of Chapter 4 with the teacher, to highlight key areas that you will focus on with your child. We have found that it is most helpful to ask teachers to prompt and praise children for working on two key skills in the classroom: writing down assignments in the DAR, and filing papers appropriately for transfer between school and home (using an accordion file, as discussed in detail in Chapter 8). Ask if the teacher is willing to support the child's use of these skills in school by prompting, praising, and monitoring these specific target goals. You can also ask the teacher which other organizational routines would be most beneficial to your child in class. You can use this discussion to determine how best to focus your joint work with the child as you start to tackle organizational skills in the school setting.

Specifically, you will be asking the teacher to do these things (page 78):

Teacher's Organization, Time Management, and Planning (OTMP) Inventory

	Never	Sometimes	Often	Always
Tracking assignments				
The child writes down assignments inconsistently.				
The child neglects to hand in assignments on the day they are due.				
The child is unprepared for tests.				
Managing materials				
It is hard for the child to find the papers he/she needs.				
The child forgets important items (e.g., books, notebooks) at home.				
The child's desk is messy.				
The child's folders/binders are disorganized.				
Time management				
The child has difficulty getting started with in-class assignments.				
The child takes a long time to complete in-class assignments.				
Task planning				
The child has trouble knowing how to start projects/assignments.				
The child has trouble creating a plan for completing tasks (e.g., writing assignments).				
The child has difficulty meeting deadlines for long-term assignments.				
The child often hands in work that is incomplete and/or messy.				

Teacher Interview
Assessing Existing Organizational Routines/Tools

This form gives a question to ask your child's teacher for each of four main areas of organization, time management, and planning that many students need support with.

KEEPING TRACK OF ASSIGNMENTS

"How do students record assignments (for example, planner, notebook, online)?"

Current method: _____

_____

Is this method working for your child?   ❑ Yes   ❑ No

If no, will the teacher allow your child to use a different method?   ❑ Yes   ❑ No

MANAGING MATERIALS

"How do students file and organize papers?"

Current method: _____

_____

Is this method working for your child?   ❑ Yes   ❑ No

If no, will the teacher allow your child to use a different method?   ❑ Yes   ❑ No

TIME MANAGEMENT

"Do you use specific methods to help students get tasks done on time (for example, timers, clocks)?"

Current method: _____

_____

Is this method working for your child?   ❑ Yes   ❑ No

If no, will the teacher allow your child to use a different method?   ❑ Yes   ❑ No

PLANNING

"Do you break larger projects down into steps for students? If so, how?"

Current method: _____

_____

Is this method working for your child?   ❑ Yes   ❑ No

If no, will the teacher allow your child to use a different method?   ❑ Yes   ❑ No

1. *Prompt* the child to perform specific target goals (these will be noted on a copy of the DAR, as discussed below, and will change as treatment progresses).

2. *Praise* the child for performing the target goals.

3. *Provide* the child with a *check* on the DAR (which translates into a point at home) for performing the target behaviors. The teacher can place a check mark with his initials at the bottom of your child's DAR page for that day to indicate that the child has met the target goals for the day.

You will then provide home points and rewards to the child, based in part on the teacher's record of whether or not your child performed the target goals.

When speaking with your child's teacher, remember how busy a teacher's day is. What with managing the needs of multiple students, preparing lessons and materials, grading assignments, and dealing with administrative demands, teachers are often working at maximum capacity every minute of the day (and often after the school day). For that reason, your request to give individual attention to your child, in the midst of a sea of other students who require the teacher's attention, may be seen as burdensome. Be sensitive to that reality: Make sure you tell the teacher that it should take only a few minutes each day to prompt and praise the child's performance of target goals and to put a check mark with initials on the DAR. Ask the teacher how you can help make this task less burdensome, by sending reminders, creating forms for documenting the child's performance, and providing support at home. Furthermore, remember to express your appreciation for your teacher's willingness to dedicate these precious few minutes to your child. This small investment of time will provide invaluable support to the child, as the child learns and practices new organizational skills.

The Daily Assignment Record:
The Link between Home and School

As mentioned above, the teacher will be able to provide a check for the child on the DAR for each target goal that the child performs in school. When you meet with the teacher, share the DAR form in Chapter 7 (page 95) and the Teacher's Guide to the DAR handout on the following page (see the end of the Contents for information on downloading and printing copies of this form and this handout). Request that the teacher follow these steps to reinforce use of the DAR:

1. Prompt the child to fill in the DAR each day.
2. Correct any errors that the child makes.
3. Put a check mark with initials on the page if the child completes the DAR accurately and does not require any corrections.

If the teacher is not comfortable with the idea of the child's using the DAR to record assignments, and would prefer that the child use the same method of recording assignments as the rest of the class, discuss with the

Teacher's Guide to the Daily Assignment Record (DAR)

Your student has been taught and practiced a new method for writing down school assignments on a form called the Daily Assignment Record, or DAR. The DAR is designed to help students keep track of their assignments and the materials they need to complete those assignments. A copy of the DAR is provided along with this handout, so you can see its basic features:

1. A space to write down homework assignments for each subject.
2. A space to check what items need to go home (e.g., textbooks, notebooks, worksheets).
3. A space to write down any other assignments or tests that are due in the future.

The first target goal will be completing the DAR. Please review your student's DAR each day, and put a check mark with your initials on the page if it is completed accurately, without your help. If there are errors, you can correct them, but then please do not provide a check mark with your initials.

Please remember the three P's:

1. **Prompt** your student to use the target skill.
2. **Praise** the student.
3. **Provide a check mark** if the student met the target behavior.

teacher how to make that method work (see Chapter 7). Just be sure to find a spot on the other assignment record where the teacher can record a check mark for successful performance. If your child is uncomfortable getting the teacher's signature on the DAR or other assignment record because it's embarrassing to do so in front of classmates, you can figure out a more subtle way to get this done. For example, the teacher can sign the planner in the course of making normal rounds around the class, or your child can arrange to drop by during a free period to get the DAR checked and initialed.

Requesting Regular Feedback

Once you have enlisted the support of your child's teacher in working on organizational skills, it's important to keep communicating regularly. Check with the teacher at regular intervals to see how successfully your child is using the various organizational skills/routines in school. Rather than waiting for quarterly grades to find out how your child is doing in school, you will be able to get immediate feedback that will help you fine-tune your work with your child and assure more continuous improvement. You may want to use a form like the Weekly Teacher Feedback Form shown on the following page, to ensure that you are constantly up to date on your child's school performance. Beyond elementary school, getting feedback every two weeks is more practical for teachers. (See the end of the Contents for information on printing copies of the form or downloading an electronic version you can e-mail to the teacher.)

Establishing Formal Assistance

If your child's organizational difficulties are related to a diagnosed condition, such as attention-deficit/hyperactivity disorder (ADHD) or a learning disorder, it might be appropriate to use what is known as a "Section 504 plan" to facilitate teacher involvement in working with your child. Many children with ADHD have such plans, which recognize their status as children with an impairing condition, usually designated in the category of "other health impairment." Such a plan provides for teaching accommodations, usually including extended time on tests, preferential seating, and the use of daily behavior report cards. If your child already has a Section 504 plan, you could suggest adding another accommodation to the established

Weekly Teacher Feedback Form

Student: _____   Teacher: _____

Please complete this form for the week starting Monday, _____
Please e-mail **at the end of the week** to: _____

1. Please check if the student turned in his/her homework for your class on the following days:

Monday	Tuesday	Wednesday	Thursday	Friday
❑ Yes	❑ Yes	❑ Yes	❑ Yes	❑ Yes
❑ No	❑ No	❑ No	❑ No	❑ No
❑ No HW due	❑ No HW due	❑ No HW due	❑ No HW due	❑ No HW due

2. Did the student complete all in-class assignments in your class this week?
   ❑ Yes   ❑ No

   If no, which of the following situations apply?

   ❑ Student did not bring materials necessary to complete assignments.

   ❑ Student was off task during classwork time.

3. Anything else I should know?

plan, relating to organizational skills development. The new accommodation could provide for daily teacher supervision of the use of organizational tools and routines, to include a few minutes' time to prompt and praise the child's use of such tools and routines. If your child does not have a Section 504 plan and you believe that one would be appropriate, speak with the school psychologist to initiate the process of establishing a plan, and to suggest the inclusion of a teacher accommodation related to support for organizational skills acquisition. With such an official plan in place, the teacher might feel more comfortable with providing the needed assistance. It should be noted that while public schools are legally bound to provide the accommodations listed on a 504 plan, private schools are not under similar obligations.

Some other students are designated as in need of special education support. For such a student, school supports are developed and listed in an individualized education program (IEP). Issues with OTMP skills are concerns for many children with IEPs. If your child already has an IEP, you can petition to have specific goals and specific teacher support provided for building OTMP skills. We recommend that you discuss this with your child's IEP chair. In our experience, a variety of school professionals have been involved in providing OTMP support to students, including learning disability specialists, school psychologists, guidance counselors, and occupational therapists.

 Troubleshooting Tip

Working flexibly with the school

Even if parents follow all the steps suggested in this chapter to encourage school involvement in their work with their children on organization, teachers are likely to vary in their level of participation. If your child's teacher is either unable to provide help in the manner we have outlined, or agrees to help but fails to follow through, discuss the situation with the teacher to find out if there is anything you can do to make it easier for the teacher to participate. If daily monitoring simply is not realistic for your child's teacher, you may want to consider modifying the in-school recording of skill use. It may be possible for a teacher to provide a weekly report on your child's use of skills, rather than daily reports. Or, if the teacher cannot be relied on to record behavior, it may be necessary instead for you to evaluate your child's in-school performance yourself by asking your child to show evidence that the skill has been used. Your child's correct recording of assignments, for example, could be verified by checking against an online homework listing.

In our work with children and families, we have found that children benefit greatly from active cooperation between parents and school staff when they are working on mastering new skills and behaviors. However, don't be discouraged if your child's teacher does not fully participate in this program, or if you can't find another member of the staff who is willing to implement the OST system in the school and to serve as your contact for your child. If you are consistent in working with your child at home, and in reinforcing the steps that your child takes to remain organized in and out of the classroom, your child will show improvement.

Moving Forward

You now have the foundation you need to start working with your child on the OST program. Do you feel confident that you're prepared?

OST Preparation Checklist

- I have a good understanding of what to expect in Parts III and IV.
- I've talked to my child about what we'll be doing, so she feels enthusiastic that the program will help her succeed at school and at home, and she doesn't feel blamed for her organizational problems.
- I understand how to use the Home Behavior Record (HBR).
- I understand the role of prompting, monitoring, praising, and rewarding my child, and I am committed to using these strategies with him.
- I've talked to my child's teacher(s) (and/or other school personnel) and gotten a commitment to help with the OST program.
- I plan to read through the whole book, to get a more comprehensive understanding of what we'll be working on, before I start to dive into teaching my child individual skills.

Part III

Organizational Skills for School Tasks

Did you skip right to this part of the book? Go back. Here's why:

Here in Part III, we'll teach you how to choose specific organizational supplies and help your child develop the skills to use them. The supplies your child uses for organizing can be compared to the tools in a carpenter's toolbox. Having the right tools is essential for the job, but if you aren't taught how to use them, they are worthless. This is why all of the chapters before this one are so important. A good sense of the reasons behind your child's organizational challenges, and an understanding of the best ways to motivate and support your child in developing organizational skills, are essential to helping your child master the tools we present here.

Personalizing Your Plan

These chapters offer very specific advice for organizational supplies and routines to use with your child. After years of working with kids who have organizational skills difficulties, and much trial and error, these are the tools we have found to be most effective for the vast majority of kids. However, this does not mean that every one of these tools is the perfect fit for *your* child. Use your knowledge of your child, and the feedback your child gives you, to make adjustments as needed. For each tool and routine, we explain why it is a smart choice for kids with organizational skills difficulties. If, for whatever reason, you and your child decide that a specific tool or routine may not work for you, we offer "Troubleshooting Tips" that point to the key features you should look for in an alternative.

An important tool in organizing school tasks is the planner that we introduce in Chapter 7. This is a simple folder or binder that contains forms for keeping track of daily homework, long-term assignments, and after-school activities. In the interests of flexibility and personalization, we offer instructions for making a handmade planner in the book's Appendix. If you want to create a more durable version, you can have a copy shop put your forms into a spiral binder. (The box at the end of the Contents provides the URL for accessing an online supplementary appendix with instructions you can take to the copy shop, as well as forms you can print out for copying and insertion in your planner.) In Chapter 7 we ask you to make your planner—or acquire one that meets our criteria and suits your child's preferences—although we'll use the tools in it one at a time, in the same way you'll help your child master all the organizational skills in this program one at a time.

If you are choosing an alternative tool or routine, the most important rule to remember is this: **Make it simple.** This means finding the organizational routine that involves the least possible number of steps to complete. The more steps an organizational system requires, the more chances your child has to skip one. For example, storing papers in a three-ring binder with section dividers may seem like a fairly simple system. Consider, though, the steps your child has to go through when given a new paper:

1. Pull binder out of bag.
2. Flip to appropriate section.
3. Punch holes in paper.
4. Open binder rings.
5. File paper.
6. Close binder rings.
7. Put binder back in bag.

None of these steps may seem particularly taxing. But when your child has received a paper just before the bell is about to ring, only has two minutes to get to the bus, and is chatting with friends, seven steps are not going to happen. He will decide to punch holes later and stuff the paper in the wrong section, and it will end up lost among the crumpled papers at the bottom of the bag. And it will inevitably be the one critical paper you and he will frantically be searching for two weeks later.

Because of all this, we have found an accordion file to be the simplest solution. The child does not need to punch any holes or open any binder rings, and in many messenger-style bags an accordion file can be kept folded open, so that it doesn't have to be dragged in and out of the bag for a paper to be filed. We'll describe this in detail in Chapter 8.

Another reason for deviating from the plan we describe here may be that your child has a system to handle a specific organizational challenge that is working well. We subscribe to an old rule: "If it ain't broke, don't fix it." Don't worry about how organized your child's system looks to you; focus on the effectiveness of that system. If your child is writing down homework assignments on loose scraps of paper, in handwriting that is completely illegible, ask yourself this: Has she ever missed a homework assignment because she forgot it had been assigned? If the answer is no, let it go. There are going to be many battles in your war on the Glitches, and it is important to pick yours wisely.

The final, and most important, aspect of personalizing your organizational plan is to allow your child to be a full and equal partner in this process. The ultimate goal is not to teach your child how to be organized when someone else is telling him exactly what to do. Instead, we want your child to learn to understand his own organizational challenges, to learn techniques that have worked well for others in his situation, and to be able to think critically about what solutions might work best for him. In our work with kids, we typically talk with them about how the specific techniques we recommend are based on our work with hundreds of children, and ask if they would be willing to give each tool a good trial. But we also remain open to their feedback throughout and make changes based on their suggestions. If children feel strongly from the outset that a particular system is not right for them, we work with each child to come up with an alternative, and then make an agreement to check in on the system's effectiveness to see if any changes need to be made. It's often helpful to have a child come up with her own criteria to determine whether a system is working. For an example of how to frame this conversation constructively, see "Constructive Conversations" below.

CONSTRUCTIVE CONVERSATIONS

PARENT: I think an accordion file might be helpful, because all of your papers will be in one place, so you'll be less likely to lose them.

Child: I really don't think that will work for me. It would be too heavy to carry all of my papers around all the time. I'd rather just use individual folders and keep the ones I don't need at school.

Parent: Do you think you might leave a folder that you need at school by accident?

Child: I wouldn't do that. I really want to use folders.

Parent: OK, sounds like it's worth a shot. Can we agree to give it a try for two weeks and see how it's working?

Child: OK.

Parent: Let's decide how we'll determine whether it's working well or we need to make a change. If the system works well, how many times do you think you will not have a paper that you need over the next two weeks?

Child: Never.

Parent: Well, even with a great system, it's hard to be perfect. How about we allow for two missing papers? If it's more than that, we'll agree to try something new. Is that OK?

Getting Started with the Home Behavior Record

As you start working on the skills in the next chapter with your child, you will begin using the Home Behavior Record (HBR), described and provided in Chapter 5. If you recall, we've mentioned that the five specific goals on the HBR will change over time as your child masters some skills and moves on to new ones. Each time we present a new skill in the following chapters, we present a corresponding new goal to include on the HBR. When you add a new goal to the HBR, you should "retire" a goal that your child has mastered (according to the mastery criteria listed at the end of each chapter). After you have removed a goal from the HBR, keep monitoring your child's use of that skill informally and praising your child when he uses it. It is entirely possible that your child might slip a little in his use of previously mastered goals over time; if that happens, you can always put the goal back into the HBR to provide extra monitoring and reinforcement.

If your child has not mastered any of the goals on the current HBR, wait to take on any new skills until one of these goals has been achieved. There is no right amount of time for completing this program. Go at your child's pace, and know that in the long term, it's best to be patient and be sure that your child is comfortable with all skills before moving on to new ones.

Time now to get started! The Glitches' days are numbered.

Parents' Roadmap through the Skills Chapters

1. READ UP on the first five skills.

2. ADD the skills as the first five goals on the Home Behavior Record (HBR).

3. TEACH the skills to your child (use "Constructive Conversations" when needed!).

4. PRACTICE with your child.

5. PROMPT and PRAISE skill use.

6. AWARD POINTS and prizes for skill use on the HBR.

7. MONITOR for when your child has met the mastery criterion for any of the skills.

8. GRADUATE that skill from the HBR and start on a new one!

9. READ UP on the new skill.

10. ADD the new skill as a goal on the HBR.

11. RETURN to Step 3 and proceed from there.

7

Tracking Assignments

Skills taught in this chapter	Tools and routines introduced
Tracking daily assignments	Daily Assignment Record (DAR)
Tracking long-term assignments	Assignment and Test Calendar (A&TC)

Glitch we are battling:
Go-Ahead-Forget It Glitch

What it says: **"You'll remember your homework. No need to write it down."**

Key strategy: **Writing it down, right away, in one consistent place.**

If there is one feeling we hear expressed time and time again by students struggling with organization, it is this: They are overwhelmed. They have so many papers, tests, deadlines, and assignments, and it feels like too much to handle. The process we outline here can be overwhelming, too—for both your child and you. So please take one step at a time and stay focused on each step, without thinking ahead to what still needs to be done. We start guiding kids down the path to organization by taking on tracking assignments. If a child does not know what the homework assignments are in the first place, then none of the other organizational skills are applicable. So, as a first step, we will help you establish a consistent place for your child to record homework, as well as a clear routine to write down every assignment, for every class, every day.

 Troubleshooting Tip

"But I don't need a planner—it's all online!"

Many schools are now posting assignments online, and this practice can be a lifesaver in many ways for students struggling with organization. However, in our experience, online assignment systems can have a number of pitfalls. Here are some key issues to consider as you decide how an online system should fit into your child's organizational routine:

■ **Inconsistency.** This is the most critical issue: The online systems in many schools are not used by 100% of the faculty for 100% of the assignments. However, because *routines* are critical for students struggling with organization, a single, consolidated system for tracking assignments is essential. If the online postings can't be that single system, we recommend having a child use a paper planner to record assignments in all classes. Writing down assignments in class needs to become a solid, ingrained habit, where students are pulling out their planners in every single class and using them the same way every time.

■ **Accessibility.** Consider whether the online system is accessible to your child at all times when he might need to know what his assignments are. If, for example, your child completes some work during a study hall or after-school program, are computers available so that he can easily look up the assigned homework?

■ **Awareness.** Physically writing down the assignment, as well as seeing it each time the planner is opened during the day, helps many students stay aware of the work to complete. This can be particularly useful for long-term assignments, where frequent reminders can prevent the all-too-common phenomenon of a project's popping up on a child's radar the night before it is due.

■ **Materials management.** Children who use an online record often wait to get home to look up their assignments. Sometimes this is too late for them to make sure they have the needed items with them. A written record that includes a reminder list of the items needed to complete the assignment is critical for getting everything home. We recommend that any assignment list include a spot for writing down the materials that are needed for those assignments.

Bottom line: Reliance on online homework postings is very attractive to most students struggling with organization, and understandably so. However, unless all teachers are committed to this system 100% of the time, the homework site is easily accessible wherever the student needs to do work, the student has a solid method for staying aware of long-term assignments, and the child never fails to bring home the needed materials or books, an old-fashioned planner or another written record is still your best bet.

Tracking Daily Assignments

Problems with Tracking Daily Assignments

The biggest problem students have with writing down daily assignments is that they simply don't do it. They are running off to the next place they need to be, and they have a Glitch telling them that they will remember what they have to do (or can always call a friend to ask about the assignment later). In addition, we've found that traditional planners are typically not set up to accommodate children with organizational difficulties. Problems with typical planners include the following:

- Inadequate space to record assignment details.
- Weekly page views, which require students to turn the page to see any upcoming long-term assignments. (Remember that we always want to **make it simple,** or take steps out of a child's organizational routine whenever possible. For a child who struggles with organization, turning a page counts as a step.)
- Lack of additional tools to help with managing materials, time management, or task planning on the planner pages.

Our Time-Tested Solution: The Daily Assignment Record

It became clear early in our work that traditional planners were not working well for our students, so we decided to create our own. This planner was tested and refined over the years, based on feedback from our students. We've included instructions for making your own version of this planner in the Appendix to this book (see the end of the Contents for information on downloading and printing copies of the Daily Assignment Record [DAR] and other forms for your child's planner). Our planner has a number of components related to different aspects of the program, such as an Afternoon Schedule bar on the DAR to help with afternoon time management, and a form called the Task-Planning Sheet, which children use when working on long-term assignment planning. You should prepare your child's whole planner now, but we will be ignoring all of the forms to be included in it except the DAR for the time being. Instruct your child to do the same. As we'll say again and again, we are taking things one step at a time, and until perfect use of the DAR is second nature, we won't be moving on to the next step.

So let's look at the DAR, which is presented on the facing page. For now, let's just look at the most basic sections of the DAR; we'll go over it in more detail in later chapters. Each day is assigned its own DAR page, to allow ample room for writing down assignments. The leftmost column lists the child's subjects, and the column immediately following ("What is the homework?") provides space to write down any homework assigned in that subject that is *due the next day*. Any new assignments that are due *more than one day in the future* are listed in the "Tests and long-term assignments" column toward the right side of the form. We make this distinction because homework due the following day is treated differently from longer-term assignments. We'll talk about this a bit more when we discuss the Assignment and Test Calendar (A&TC) below.

The two columns to the right of the "What is the homework?" column contain checklists where your child can mark off the items he will need to bring home to complete his homework for a given subject, and the things he should bring back to school the next day. Technically, this is an aspect of materials management, which we cover in Chapter 8. We include it here, though, because it is helpful for your child to learn to do this step in conjunction with writing down her assignments: As soon as she hears what she needs to do that afternoon, she should be thinking about what materials she will need to do it.

 Troubleshooting Tip

What if your child doesn't want to use the DAR or other parts of our planner?

We have tested the DAR and other elements of our planner, and have found these effective with hundreds of children, but no tool will work if your child doesn't buy into its use. Kids occasionally object to a given solution for a variety of reasons; for instance, they may not like having a planner that stands out as different from the one their classmates are using. If your child decides he would like to use a different planner, try to find one that has as many of the features on page 96 as possible:

Daily Assignment Record (DAR)

Date: _____

Subject	What is the homework?	What do I need to take home?	What do I need to take to class tomorrow?	Tests and long-term assignments		Afternoon schedule
				Assignment	Due	*Write in 15- to 30-minute time slots below when you will likely be doing homework*
	Done? ☐	— Worksheets — Workbook — Textbook — Notebook Other: ___	— Worksheets — Workbook — Textbook — Notebook Other: ___			**WHAT** is there to do? (Check DAR & A&TC.) **HOW LONG** will it take? **WHEN** can I fit it in?
	Done? ☐	— Worksheets — Workbook — Textbook — Notebook Other: ___	— Worksheets — Workbook — Textbook — Notebook Other: ___			
	Done? ☐	— Worksheets — Workbook — Textbook — Notebook Other: ___	— Worksheets — Workbook — Textbook — Notebook Other: ___			
	Done? ☐	— Worksheets — Workbook — Textbook — Notebook Other: ___	— Worksheets — Workbook — Textbook — Notebook Other: ___			
	Done? ☐	— Worksheets — Workbook — Textbook — Notebook Other: ___	— Worksheets — Workbook — Textbook — Notebook Other: ___			

REMINDER! Announcements or special papers		— Handouts
		Other: ___
			— Handouts
			Other: ___
						Started HW:
						  Early/on time/late
						Finished HW:
						  Early/on time/late

From *The Organized Child* by Richard Gallagher, Elana G. Spira, and Jennifer L. Rosenblatt. Copyright © 2018 The Guilford Press. Purchasers of this book can photocopy and/or download enlarged versions of this material (see the box at the end of the table of contents).

95

- Ample space for writing down assignments in appropriate detail.
- Space to make note of any materials that need to come home to complete the assignment, and materials that need to return to school the next day.
- A method for distinguishing assignments due the next day from longer-term assignments.

If your child wants to use a different planner, try to find one that also includes the following advantages of the monthly-view Assignment and Test Calendar (see below):

- It allows for a long-term view of upcoming assignments.
- It's visible on a daily basis, without the need to turn any pages.

Our planner contains other components: a weekly schedule or Personal Calendar (see Chapter 9) and a Task-Planning Sheet for long-term planning (see Chapter 10). Before you and your child select an alternative planner, it may be helpful to review the key features of these components in their respective chapters, to help guide you to an option that mimics these functions as well as possible.

THE ROUTINE

Sit down with your child and review the features of the DAR. Explain to your child that effective use of the DAR depends on developing a solid routine to be used in exactly the same way each time an assignment is given:

- The child's planner should be *out and open* (with the DAR plainly visible) on your child's desk in any situation where homework may be assigned.
- Your child should listen carefully to decide whether an assignment is *short-term* (due the next day) or *long-term* (due in two days or more).
- Any short-term assignments should be listed in the "What is the homework?" column of the DAR in appropriate detail.
- Any long-term assignments should be listed in the "Tests and long-term assignments" column, along with their due dates.
- **Critical step:** If your child has no homework to list for a given subject, she should mark down "None" or put an "×" through the box (this is true for both the short- and long-term assignment columns). This is essential for two reasons: (1) If a box is left blank, it is unclear whether this means that there is actually no homework or that your

child forgot to record it; and (2) you will want to have your child develop the strong habit of having the planner out and writing something down for every school subject, every single time.

- Your child should check off any materials that should be brought home to complete the assignment, and any materials that should be returned to school the next day, in the two "What do I need . . . ?" columns.

- At the end of the evening, when homework is complete, your child should rip out that day's DAR page. We suggest this so that your child will not have to rifle through old DAR pages to get to the one he needs for a particular day. Additionally, if you're using a planner made at a copy center, removing the DAR that has been used allows the child to see a monthly calendar on the other side of the folder. This calendar (the Assignment and Test Calendar) is an important feature, which we'll discuss later in this chapter when we talk about tracking long-term assignments.

 Troubleshoot

One thing at a time

Children who struggle with organization are sometimes impulsive or have difficulty focusing on the task at hand. If your child wants to dive in and try to use all the features of the planner at once, emphasize that you're talking only about the DAR right now. If you have read ahead, feel free to give her a brief preview, but we strongly recommend having her start out by only using the DAR. It's tempting to capitalize on her enthusiasm, but taking on too much at once often leads to failure. Instead, use her excitement to motivate her to master this step so that she can move on to the next.

PRACTICE

Run through a few practice sessions, in which you pretend to be one of your child's teachers and your child actually uses the DAR to write down the assignments. Try to mimic your child's typical assignments, as well as the way in which assignments are usually announced (on the board, orally, online, etc.). Also, be sure to throw in some challenges. Assign a mix of short- and long-term assignments to your child without explicitly labeling them as such. Prod him to hurry because the bell is about to ring.

After each "day" of assignments you give, check your child's work. Be a stickler for details. If today is Monday and you said something was due Wednesday, is it in the "Tests and long-term assignments" column? If you "assigned" a worksheet, did your child check off that she needed to bring a worksheet home and take it back to school for that subject? Did the child write down all of the important details? Is something written in every single box, even if it is just "None" or an "×"? Keep going until your child writes down three consecutive "days" of assignments with 100% accuracy and no prompts from you.

Unfortunately, one of the most difficult aspects of this routine is hard to practice at home: remembering to pull out the planner and use the DAR when it is needed in each class. If your child has a teacher willing to help, asking the teacher to prompt your child to take out the planner and use the DAR can be very helpful.

REWARDING DAR USE

Once you and your child have finished practice with the DAR, you are ready to start implementing the Home Behavior Record (HBR; see Chapter 5). Remember that it is best to set aside some time each afternoon or evening to review the points your child has earned on the HBR and provide praise.

As we have discussed before, your child will always have five goals on her HBR. Once she has mastered a skill, you can remove it from the HBR and substitute the next one.

To get started, use the following five goals, which are the first five goals listed in the Mastery Worksheet at the end of this chapter:

1. Brings home planner from school.
2. Has DAR page completed with 100% accuracy.
3. Obtains teacher's check mark with initials, indicating that assignments were written down correctly.
4. Follows the homework rules.
5. Participates in nightly check-in cooperatively (is cooperative in sitting down with you and letting you check on and review points each evening).

We'll discuss the second and third goals in a bit more detail here.

GOAL

Has DAR page completed with 100% accuracy.

When your child comes home from school, look over the DAR for the day. To earn a point for 100% accuracy, your child should have:

- Something filled out in each box, even if it is "none" or an "×."
- Assignments written down, with all important details listed.
- Materials checklists checked off appropriately.
- Short-term and long-term assignments recorded in their proper columns.

Your child should receive a point only if **every single one of these requirements is met perfectly**. Even the smallest error means no point that day. This stance may sound harsh, but there is an important scientific basis for it: When we reward behaviors, those behaviors increase. If we reward perfect planner use, perfect planner use will increase. But if we reward almost-perfect planner use, then the behavior that will increase is almost-perfect planner use. And sometimes those small mistakes that make the planner less than perfect can have big consequences. A small error in recording the date to dress up for a History class presentation, for example, could lead to a very unhappy Abraham Lincoln sitting in the front row of the class picture. That being said, while you need to be stingy with points, you can and should always be generous and encouraging with your praise. See the "Constructive Conversations" example below to get an idea of how this feedback could go.

CONSTRUCTIVE CONVERSATIONS

Parent: Wow. Your DAR for today looks amazing. You wrote down an assignment or "None" in each box; you put all the details down; and you checked off all the materials you needed. This took a lot of work—what a fantastic job! Oh, no—there's just one small mistake.

Child: What mistake?

Parent: Look at this poem for Language Arts. You wrote that it's due the day after tomorrow, but you put it in the "What is the homework?" column. It should be over here in the "Tests and long-term assignments" column.

Child: I *knew* that. I just had to write it down quickly, so I made a mistake. Everything else is perfect, though. Can I *please* have the point?

Parent: The point is for when it is 100% perfect, and I know you will get there. I mean, look how amazingly you did, and we just got started! I really can't tell you how proud I am. To be this close to perfection so early is a big accomplishment.

In addition to having the child fill out the DAR correctly, you will want to know that the child has written down the assignments accurately. Monitoring this behavior can be a bit of a challenge. If you have a teacher (or other school "point person") who is willing and able to work with you on the program, you can ask that teacher to check off and initial the student's planner to indicate that the assignments were written down correctly. (For a child who changes classes, it is sufficient to have one teacher initial that the assignment for that class is recorded accurately.) Ask the teacher to put a check mark with initials on the DAR *only if your child wrote down the assignment correctly on his own.* If the assignment was written down incorrectly, ask the teacher to make a correction, but not to check off or initial the DAR. (A side note: If the teacher is willing, it is fine for him to remind your child that the DAR needs to be checked. Your child is taking on a lot of new responsibilities right now, and it isn't necessary to make remembering to ask the teacher about this an additional one.)

 HBR GOAL

Obtains teacher's check mark with initials, indicating that assignments were written down correctly.

If your child does not have a teacher who is participating in the program, there are a couple of options for alternative goals to use in the HBR. First, if your child's school uses an online system for posting assignments, you can use this system to check the assignments your child writes down each day. Your child earns a point if all of the assignments listed on the DAR match those posted online. If this is not an option, feel free to substitute any other means of checking the homework's accuracy you may have at your disposal (like checking with a classmate's parent). If no accuracy check is possible, you can reward your child for using the planner for this day and check with the teacher about general accuracy at a later time to see if your child is completing the appropriate homework. If your child has been inaccurate, then you could request that the teacher get more directly involved on a daily basis.

Now you have taught your child the first OST program skills, and your next job is to be patient. Stick with these skills until your child has mastered at least one of them (see the Mastery Worksheet at the end of this chapter). Once she has reached that point, you can move on to the next section.

Tracking Long-Term Assignments

Problems with Tracking Long-Term Assignments

Long-term assignments are often the bane of existence for the parent of a child struggling with organizational skills. If your child is too young to have many long-term assignments yet, it's important to know that these pose major challenges to children as they get older, so helping your child develop skills to deal with them early is critical. We break our battle with long-term assignments into two pieces: knowing what they are and getting them done. We'll deal with the first piece now and the second in Chapter 9.

As we've mentioned before, a key problem with traditional planners is that when students write long-term assignments down on their due dates (if they write them down at all), the assignments become immediately invisible, unless the students flip forward in the pages. Typically, students don't turn the page forward until that week arrives, leading to last-minute panic about getting work done.

Our Time-Tested Solution: The Assignment and Test Calendar

The Assignment and Test Calendar, shown on page 103, is simply a monthly-view calendar where your child can list long-term assignments on their due dates. You and your child will also use this calendar to help plan the completion of long-term projects, but we won't get to that until Chapter 10. The thing that makes the Assignment and Test Calendar special, though, is how it is structured within the planner. When your child opens the planner, the calendar is always in view, providing a constant reminder of the assignments on the horizon.

THE ROUTINE

First, set up an Assignment and Test Calendar page for the current month. Fill in the blank for the month at the top of the form, and then fill in the days (use a standard calendar for the current month as a guide). Now, every time your child lists an assignment in the "Tests and long-term assignments" column of the DAR, that assignment should be written on the Assignment and Test Calendar on the day it is due. This can be done in one of two ways:

Option 1: Your child can immediately transfer the information onto the Assignment and Test Calendar after writing it in the DAR. Caution: Constraints during class time often make this difficult.

Option 2: She can transfer the information as the first part of her routine when she sits down and opens her planner to start homework in the afternoon.

In either event, at the start of homework, your child should mark a large "X" through the current day of the Assignment and Test Calendar. This is meant to indicate that your child has checked to see if any assignments were given that day that need to be recorded in the Assignment and Test Calendar, and also that she has looked over this calendar to see what due dates are approaching. (See the end of the Contents for information on downloading and printing copies of the Assignment and Test Calendar, and the book's Appendix and the supplemental online appendix for instructions on including it in your child's planner.)

PRACTICE

You and your child can practice use of the Assignment and Test Calendar in conjunction with some extra DAR practice. Give your child a new round of assignments, in the same way you did when he was learning the DAR. Then, at the end of each "day," have your child pretend to sit down and start homework. Have him open his planner and transfer all assignments to the Assignment and Text Calendar (in light pencil—and be sure to erase the fake ones when you are done!). Then have him look over this calendar and make an "×" through the current day. Do this until he has completed three trials with 100% accuracy.

Assignment and Test Calendar (A&TC)

What Is due? *Look to your daily assignment record*

Month: _____

Sunday	Monday	Tuesday	Wednesday	Thursday	Friday	Saturday	Steps for Planning a Long-Term Assignment/Test
Done? ☐	Done? ☐	Done? ☐	Done? ☐	Done? ☐	Done? ☐	Done? ☐	☐ What steps do I need to take? ☐ What stuff do I need? ☐ How long will each step take? ☐ Fit it in: Write the steps in your A&TC ↩ ☐ Check it out: Is it done neatly and completely?
Done? ☐	Done? ☐	Done? ☐	Done? ☐	Done? ☐	Done? ☐	Done? ☐	
Done? ☐	Done? ☐	Done? ☐	Done? ☐	Done? ☐	Done? ☐	Done? ☐	REMINDER!
Done? ☐	Done? ☐	Done? ☐	Done? ☐	Done? ☐	Done? ☐	Done? ☐	
Done? ☐	Done? ☐	Done? ☐	Done? ☐	Done? ☐	Done? ☐	Done? ☐	

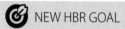 ENHANCING SUCCESS

If the thought of more practice with using forms makes you want to pull your hair out, do whatever you can to stick with it without expressing aggravation. Using the DAR and the Assignment and Test Calendar every day probably makes your child want to pull her hair out too. The point of all this practice is to make using these forms a mindless routine. Some things are just boring, but if we keep doing them, we can get used to that boredom. You and your child will also get faster the more you practice. You can provide extra praise for this practice; you can also say frankly to your child, "I know that doing this over and over again may seem annoying, but I appreciate your effort."

REWARDING ASSIGNMENT AND TEST CALENDAR USE

Now is the time to make your first change to the HBR. Remove the goal your child has mastered to the greatest extent—see the Mastery Worksheet at the end of this chapter (and let him know he has graduated from his first goal!). If the child starts to backslide on the goal once it has been removed, you can always put it back into the HBR. In the empty spot, add a goal involving the use of the Assignment and Test Calendar. This is the highlighted "NEW" goal on this Mastery Worksheet. (Note, however, that in the Mastery Worksheets for Chapters 8, 9, and 10, *all* of the goals will be new goals, and so this highlighted row will not appear.)

NEW HBR GOAL

Transfers all long-term assignments to the Assignment and Test Calendar, and crosses off the current day.

Again, remember to be a stickler, albeit a warm, encouraging one!

Take a Breath!

Continue to take things slowly, and once your child has really mastered all of the skills on this new HBR, you will have successfully beaten the Go-Ahead-Forget-It Glitch! Be sure to congratulate both your child and yourself. These victories often seem huge before they are begun and small once they've been completed, but it's essential to be sure that you let your child know what a big challenge he has overcome. Feel free to have fun with this. You could buy four little figures to represent each of the Glitches. Once your child has mastered the skills in each chapter, you can have a ceremony banishing the Glitch you've just beaten to a shoebox Glitch cave.

 Tip for Older Children

Older kids might earn an official Glitch Conqueror certificate once each section is done. Throw around ideas with your child and get creative!

But when your celebrating is done, gear yourself up, because the Go-Ahead-Lose-It Glitch is preparing for battle . . .

Use the Mastery Worksheet on the following page to keep track of which goals your child has mastered. Once the first goal your child has mastered is checked off, be sure to add the new one to your child's HBR (see Chapter 5). Check off these goals as your child masters them, replacing the first one mastered with the new goal of transferring long-term assignments to the Assignment and Test Calendar.

 ENHANCING SUCCESS

Being reminded of their accomplishments is very motivating to most kids, so consider keeping your child's Mastery Worksheets together: Staple them together as they accumulate, or even tack them up in a column on a door or wall, so that you can point to the child's accomplishments whenever he needs a boost—"Look how much you've accomplished already!"—or so that he'll just see them as he walks by.

Mastery Worksheet
Chapter 7 Goals for the Home Behavior Record

Goal	Mastery criterion	Mastered?
Brings home planner from school.	Two weeks of bringing home planner all five days.	
Has DAR page completed with 100% accuracy.	Two weeks of completing page with no errors.	
Obtains teacher's check mark with initials, indicating that assignments were written down correctly.	Two weeks of getting teacher's initials every day.	
Follows the homework rules.	Two weeks of following the homework rules.	
Participates in nightly check-in cooperatively (is cooperative in sitting down with you and letting you check on and review points each evening).	One week of cooperative check-ins.	
NEW: Transfers all long-term assignments to the Assignment and Test Calendar, and crosses off the current day.	Two weeks of transferring assignments/crossing off day perfectly with no prompting.	

8

Managing School Materials

Skills taught in this chapter	Tools and routines introduced
Managing papers	Accordion file "Weed It Out" Hanging file box
Managing backpacks	Backpack checklist Containers and compartments
Using lockers effectively (for middle school and beyond)	Locker shelf Locker checklist

Glitch we are battling:
Go-Ahead-Lose-It Glitch

What it says: **"Just put it anywhere. You'll remember where it is."**

Key strategy: **Having a place for everything, and putting everything back in its place as soon as you are finished with it.**

In this chapter we take on one of the biggest enemies of organization: stuff. The collection of crumb-covered papers crumpled in the bottom of your child's backpack. The book that required a 9:00 P.M. drive back to school and the mercy of a friendly custodian to retrieve. The three-month-old sandwich that lives underneath three misplaced winter coats in your child's locker. This Glitch is pervasive, so you and your child will need several solutions to battle it, but they all share a common underlying strategy. Every single piece of "stuff" your child handles should have an identified home. Things should be taken out only when they are being used, and should then be returned immediately afterward. The solutions described below are what we have found to be the best "homes" for the materials your child is expected to manage.

 ENHANCING SUCCESS

Managing school materials requires mastering more new routines than any other organizational challenge. It is especially important here to remember that these routines should be taken on **one at a time.** Remember to wait until your child has met the mastery criterion for at least one goal (see the Mastery Worksheet at the end of each chapter) before removing that goal from the Home Behavior Record (HBR) and taking on a new one.

Managing Papers

Problems with Managing Papers

For most kids, papers are the most challenging materials they have to organize. They receive many of them each day; the papers are easily damaged or destroyed; and losing just one of them can have a significant impact on their grades. A number of problems come into play when children are trying to keep papers organized:

- It can be difficult for kids to remember to have the right paper with them at the time they need it.
- Papers are often handed out when kids are in a rush to get somewhere else and don't have time to file them properly.
- Papers can easily fall out of folders and get lost or damaged.

Your child may not receive many papers if the school uses online files and an online process for turning in assignments. We discuss important routines for managing these files later in this chapter, because these files can often get lost in online space, just as physical papers are misplaced or lost.

Our Time-Tested Solution: The Accordion File

We have found that the children we see have the greatest success organizing their papers with a sturdy plastic accordion file. Look for one with at least one pocket for each of your child's school subjects, plus an extra section for papers that need to be brought home. Some accordion files have a pocket

on the outside, which can be a useful place to store pens, pencils, and other small supplies. Watch out for pockets made of mesh, though; we've found that they rarely stand up to more than a couple weeks of use. Also, try to find one with divider tabs that rise well above the papers. If the tabs are difficult to see once the file is filled, filing mistakes become more likely.

Accordion file.

🏆 ENHANCING SUCCESS

We'll talk more about choosing the right backpack for your child in a bit, but for students who struggle with paper management, an accordion file coupled with a messenger-style backpack can be a great solution. When stored in a messenger bag, an accordion file can be kept folded open, allowing a child to file papers directly in the bag, without having to pull the accordion file in and out. This is a great way to **make it simple:** Take a step out of your child's organizational routine.

To set up his accordion file, have your child label the section tabs with the names of each of his subjects. As the final section tab label, have him write "For Parents." This section is the place for announcements, permission slips, or other papers that need your attention. Brainstorm with your child to see if there are any papers he receives that would not fit into either a subject section or a "For Parents" section, and then create new sections as needed. We recommend avoiding a "Miscellaneous" section, because this tends to become a catch-all that rarely gets looked at. (See the "Constructive Conversations" example below for advice on creating effective section labels with your child.) If your accordion file comes with stickers to label the section tabs, throw them out; we find that stickers fall off quickly when the file is being used. Instead, have your child use a permanent marker to write subjects directly on the tabs.

CONSTRUCTIVE CONVERSATIONS

Parent: OK, you've written all your subjects on section tabs, and we have a "For Parents" section. Do you think we're missing anything?

Child: I can't think of anything.

Parent: Let's look at the binder you're using now and see if there are any sections we're forgetting.

Child: I have a section for "Art" in my old binder, but we don't really get any papers in Art class, so I don't think I need a section for that in my accordion file.

Parent: OK. Now let's look at the loose papers in your backpack and see if we would have a place to file all of them in the accordion file. Where would this one go?

Child: Hmm. That's a copy of the cafeteria menu for this week. I don't know which section I would put that in. Maybe I could make a section called "Announcements."

When we work with kids to set up their files, we like to give them a pack of colored permanent markers and let them write their subjects on the section tabs, using whatever colors they choose for each subject. Then we spend time letting them decorate and personalize their files, using stickers, paint pens, and other arts and crafts materials. This may seem like an unimportant step, but letting children take pride in and ownership of their organizational system can be very helpful in motivating them to organize.

 Troubleshooting Tip

What to look for if you need an alternative to the accordion file

These are the features that make the accordion file work well for kids who have trouble organizing papers. If you decide to try an alternative solution, try to look for one that has as many of these features as possible:

- All papers are in one place, so as long as the child has the file, she will have the papers she needs.
- Unlike individual folders, the sides of the file are *closed*, which prevents papers from falling out.
- The process of putting papers into the file is *quick*—there are no holes to punch, binder rings to open, or sections to flip through.

THE ROUTINE

First, have your child make a decision as to whether papers in each section of the accordion file should go before the divider for that section or after, and stick with it. This takes some time to get used to, so it is important to be consistent. Next, teach your child the basic principles of using the accordion file:

- All papers should go in their proper sections *as soon as they are received.*

- The child should take papers out only when they are needed.

- Papers should be put back in their proper sections *as soon as the child is finished using them.*

PRACTICE

You can use the chore of transferring papers from your child's old organizational system to the accordion file as an opportunity for your child to practice using the new system. Take papers from different subjects, and pretend to be your child's teacher handing them out. Have your child practice filing them quickly. Do some practices where your child has to file papers under time pressure because it's the end of the school day. Ask your child about the real challenges he faces in filing during the school day, and try to mimic those situations during practice. Then help your child practice taking a paper out (such as a worksheet to complete for homework) and returning it to the appropriate section *immediately* after he uses it.

REWARDING PAPER MANAGEMENT

When your child begins working on paper management, you can add two new goals to the HBR (see the Mastery Worksheet at the end of this chapter for all the new goals for managing materials). The first involves checking on the state of your child's backpack when she arrives home:

 NEW HBR GOAL

Has all papers filed in correct sections of accordion file, with no loose papers in backpack.

To monitor this goal, begin checking your child's backpack each afternoon or evening after you have looked over her DAR. Quickly look through her accordion file and see if you notice any papers filed in the wrong sections. (This is also a good time to look in the "For Parents" section for anything that you might need to review.) As always with goals on the HBR, it's best to be very strict when awarding points, while being encouraging and understanding in your attitude and praise. This means that even if all papers are filed perfectly in the accordion file and your child's backpack looks neater than it has in ages, but there is a solitary permission slip sitting in the bottom of your child's bag, she should not receive her point. If the boundaries around the criteria for earning points are blurry, it is natural for kids to try to push those lines as far as they can. However, you should heap on the praise, remind her how proud you are of her progress, and let her know you are confident she is on her way to earning her point the next day.

If you have a teacher who is willing to provide you with information about your child's organizational skill use at school, you can add a second new goal:

 NEW HBR GOAL

Receives teacher point for filing all papers correctly during class.

For this point, ask your child's teacher to watch your child whenever papers are passed out in class and see if he files papers in the accordion file. Don't ask the teacher to monitor whether papers are being put in the right sections, which would be asking for too much of her time. It's fine if your child requires a prompt to carry out this procedure at first. The teacher should sign the DAR at the end of the day to indicate that all papers were placed in the accordion file.

Managing Backpacks

Problems with Managing Backpacks

Once papers have been successfully tamed, the greatest part of the backpack battle has typically been won. With all papers neatly filed and easily found, two key problems remain for your child:

- Making sure that everything that needs to come home is put in the backpack before leaving school, and that everything that needs to go to school is put in the backpack before leaving home.

- Finding homes for all items in the backpack that are not papers.

We'll take on each issue in turn. First up: Helping your child remember to pack her backpack with everything she needs for home and school.

Our Time-Tested Solution: The Backpack Checklist

Checklists are great tools for battling the Go-Ahead-Lose-It Glitch. We have found that checklists work particularly well for packing backpacks. Our backpack checklist consists of an index card, which we place inside a plastic name badge protector (available at most office supply stores). On the index card, we make large check boxes and list the essential items each child needs to remember when packing her bag. Then we use extra-large safety pins to pin the checklist inside the bag. We usually attach it to the upper back of the inside of the backpack so that it is clearly visible whenever the backpack is open.

When making the backpack checklist, sit down with your child and brainstorm what he would like to include. Some items that are commonly needed include textbooks, notebooks, planner, accordion file, pen/pencil case, lunch, gym clothes, library books, keys, money, phone, musical instruments, and cards for public transportation. Once you have decided on the best items to include, give your child the index card and some colored markers, and allow him to list these in the order and colors that make the most sense to him. Don't make the list too long. We have found that most children can cover their needs with six or seven items.

After your child has been practicing using the checklist for a while, the colors associated with each item may be sufficient

Backpack checklist.

to trigger her memory. Some students find it useful to have a second, short-hand reminder attached to the zipper of their bags that includes only the color codes for each item. This reminder can be created on a manila tag, with a colored dot corresponding to each item. Alternatively, embroidery threads in each item's color can be tied directly to the backpack's zipper.

 Troubleshooting Tip

What to look for if you need an alternative to a backpack checklist

These are the features that make the backpack checklist work well in helping kids remember needed items. If you decide to try an alternative solution, try to look for one that has as many of these features as possible:

- Each needed item is clearly presented in a format that is *easy to read* quickly.
- The checklist is always visible when the child is packing/unpacking, as a *visual cue* to remember to check for everything the child needs.
- The checklist is in a *sturdy* protector that can withstand being jostled with other items in the backpack.

 Troubleshooting Tip

Staying on top of a letter-day schedule

We've found that rotating, letter-day schedules are particular challenges for children with organizational skills difficulties. On this type of schedule, your child might need different items on different days (for example, gym clothes on A and C days only). The backpack checklist can be used to help your child stay on top of these requirements—for instance, "A or C day → Bring gym clothes." If your child has difficulty keeping track of what letter day it is, you can help your child fill in the letter days on the Assignment and Test Calendar at the beginning of each month. Then encourage your child to check the calendar each evening after homework is completed to see what letter day is coming up, and to use the backpack checklist to make sure that all needed items are packed.

THE ROUTINE

When packing up to go home for the day from school, or packing up at home at the end of homework, your child should go through the checklist item by item and check to see whether each item is in her bag. It is useful, particularly when she is first becoming accustomed to this routine, for your child to go through this process out loud with you when she is packing up at home. Sit with her and listen as she ticks off each item and looks to see if she has remembered to put it in her bag.

PRACTICE

After initially creating the backpack checklist, sit with your child and have him pack and unpack his backpack a few times, using the checklist. Ask him to simulate the times he might be using the checklist. For example, you might first ask him to pretend he is in a math lesson, and ask him to take out all the things he would need and put them on his desk. Then tell him the bell has rung and he needs to pack his backpack. Have him think aloud as he goes through the list to pack up. Be sure to do practices that cover all the different scenarios when he will need to pack his bag (after homework at home, at the end of the school day, etc.).

 Tip for Older Children

The process of packing a backpack is more challenging for older students who change classes throughout the day. In this case, have your child practice packing up to move from one class to the next, and include some time pressure in your simulation. The easiest way to forget something is when a child is moving quickly to make it to the next class, so it is important for your child to think ahead about how he is going to handle this situation.

REWARDING CHECKLIST USE

Your child can receive an at-home point on the HBR for packing up her backpack for the night in front of you. She should use the checklist and verbalize as she goes through each item.

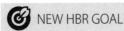 NEW HBR GOAL

Uses backpack checklist when packing backpack at night.

Once your child becomes skilled at having all the things he needs in his backpack when he needs them, you and he can fine-tune his organization even further, by making sure that each of these items is easy for him to locate.

Our Time-Tested Solution: Containers and Compartments

The best strategy for organizing all items in the backpack is a straightforward application of the principle that guides all of the solutions in this chapter: Everything should have its own home and be returned immediately to its home after use. The key exercise here is to identify specific places for each item in your child's backpack, using containers and compartments. Sit down with your child, and take an inventory together of all the things that need to go into her backpack and all of the different pockets and sections of her backpack. Ask her to go through and decide which item should go with which compartment. Also, decide whether any containers, such as pencil cases, may be useful.

 Troubleshooting Tip

Solving the mystery of the missing pencil case

Pencil cases are the most commonly misplaced items in backpacks. If your child's pencil case frequently goes missing, try using a soft-sided case and attaching it directly to the inside of the backpack. You can sew a ribbon to the case and attach the other end to your child's backpack, or use an oversized safety pin to pin the case inside.

If your child's backpack does not have sufficient compartments to separate all of the different things he needs to carry, the two of you may decide that a new backpack would be a better solution. Take note of the things he needs to separate and their sizes, and look for a backpack with compartments to match these needs. As we've mentioned above in the section on paper management section, a messenger-style bag may be a good solution if your child finds it tiresome to take an accordion file in and out of the backpack each time he needs to file a paper. With a messenger-style bag, the accordion file can be kept folded open, and the papers can be filed directly into the bag. *The key function of all containers and compartments is that they provide each item with its own unique and easily accessible place in your child's backpack.*

THE ROUTINE

To use containers and compartments effectively, your child needs to memorize the sections she has assigned for each item. The real work lies in developing this habit: The moment your child is done with a given item, it should go directly back to its place. It is very easy for the Go-Ahead-Lose-It Glitch to creep in here and say, "Just leave it out; you're busy and you can put it in later," or "Throw it in the bag—you can organize before you go home." Talk with your child about these traps, and ask how she plans to avoid them.

PRACTICE

Mimic the practice for the backpack checklist described above. This time, emphasize your child's putting all supplies away in their proper place.

REWARDING CONTAINER AND COMPARTMENT USE

When your child is ready, you can modify his backpack checklist goal to include the use of containers and compartments. When you do your backpack checklist check, also take note of whether or not your child has put each item into his backpack in its designated place.

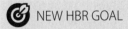 NEW HBR GOAL

Uses backpack checklist when packing backpack at night, and puts all backpack items in designated containers and compartments.

If your child's teacher is helping you track her organizational skill use at school, you can add a second goal to the HBR, assessing the combined effects of all the materials management skills she has learned to this point:

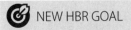 NEW HBR GOAL

Received teacher point for having all necessary papers and supplies in class.

Managing Long-Term Paper Storage

Problems with Long-Term Paper Storage

Once all systems are well in place to keep your child's backpack under control, it is a good time to revisit paper storage. If your child has been doing a good job of using the accordion file system for a while, you will inevitably run into a new problem: The file will become filled to capacity with papers, making it difficult for your child to file new papers and heavy to lug around. This is a good opportunity to teach a new set of skills: sorting through papers to determine which are necessary to keep, and developing a system for long-term storage.

Our Time-Tested Solution: The Hanging File and "Weed It Out"

We recommend setting a regular time to sit with your child and help him go through his accordion file, using a procedure we call "Weed It Out." When your child weeds out his accordion file, he takes out each paper in his file and asks himself the questions in this decision tree:

Will I ever need this paper again?	
(Double-check any "no" answers here with your child. Ask these questions: "Could this be useful for studying for finals? Is this something that you are particularly proud of? Is it possible you will need this to check your grade calculations at the end of the semester?")	
YES ↰ **Do I need to have access to it during class?**	NO ↱ **Throw it out!**
YES ↰ **Leave it in the accordion file** NO ↱ **File away in long-term storage**	

Hanging file.

For papers your child chooses to put in long-term storage, we recommend using a desktop hanging file. Include one hanging file for each section of your child's accordion file. Matching the colors of the files to the colors of the section names in the accordion file can also be helpful. Papers can be moved directly from the section of the accordion file to the corresponding section of the hanging file.

 Troubleshooting Tip

Does your child need something other than a hanging file?

If for some reason you need to use an alternative to a hanging file, be sure it has the following features:

- Papers are easily filed.
- Sections correspond perfectly with sections of accordion file, making filing and retrieval straightforward.

THE ROUTINE

The first step is to decide with your child how often the "Weed It Out" procedure is needed. This will be determined by the number of papers your child receives and how often papers are received. For a typical student, "Weed It Out" sessions can be spaced between two weeks and a month apart. Remembering to do something that occurs so infrequently can be a challenge for any student, particularly one who struggles with organizational skills. For this reason, we recommend that parents take on the responsibility of initiating "Weed It Out" sessions with their children. During a session, sit with your child and go through each paper in her file. Have her go through the decision tree above for each paper, to determine whether it should remain in the accordion file, move into the hanging file, or be thrown out.

PRACTICE

Your initial "Weed It Out" session can serve as practice for learning this skill. Have your child think aloud while going through the decision tree, and ask critical questions to clarify his thought process or raise points he may not have considered. Once the initial "Weed It Out" session has been completed, you can hold additional practice sessions using sample papers (search online for printable worksheets). You can mark some worksheets as already graded, or date them as a few months old, to help give your child clues to decide whether or not he should keep it. Holding a practice session each day for a week should give your child a good level of familiarity with the procedure.

REWARDING "WEED IT OUT"

For the week that you conduct "Weed It Out" practice sessions with your child, you can add a point to the HBR for cooperatively participating in these practices. Your child receives the point for engaging in practice even if she makes mistakes.

NEW HBR GOAL

Practices "Weed It Out" with ten sample papers.

Managing Lockers

(If your child doesn't have a locker, skip to the next section.)

Problems with Managing Lockers

A parent often shivers at the thought of what a child's locker must look like: the black hole that is in all probability the resting place of many a missing Tupperware container, sweaty gym outfit, and science fair project. If your child feels comfortable with having you participate in it, a locker cleanout is a great task for you to tackle together after school, armed with a large garbage bag, a container for taking missing items home, and some cleaning supplies. If your child would prefer to keep you out of her locker, set her up with the techniques discussed here and some supplies, and ask her to give it a try on her own.

Our Time-Tested Solutions: Locker Shelves and the Locker Checklist

The first step in organizing a locker is to pull out every item and decide what belongs in there, what should be taken home, and what should be thrown out. Once this is done, the next task is to find a structured way to store each item that belongs in the locker.

In keeping with the concept of having an identified place for all items, we find that a locker shelf can be useful for creating organized spaces in a locker. Many students find it helpful to

Locker shelf.

keep books needed before lunch on the top of the shelf, and those that are needed after lunch below the shelf. Discuss with your child the system that makes the most sense to him. The key point is that every item that belongs in his locker should have a specific, identified home.

After this, we want to come up with a system to help ensure your child remembers to take all items he needs out of the locker when he needs them. For this, we recommend the use of a locker checklist taped to the inside of the locker door. Similar to the backpack checklist, this list details each item your child needs to take with him each time he visits his locker. A typical student might need a list for what he has to pack at the start of the day, at lunch, and at the end of the day. Ask your child when he visits his locker and what he needs to remember to take with him on each trip. A Locker Checklist form is provided on page 123 for use as a template. Work with your child to create his checklist at home, and then pack it for him to take into school, along with a roll of clear packing tape to attach the list to the inside of his locker. If your child's classes vary by the day of the week, or by a letter-day schedule, you can make smaller versions for each day. (See the end of the Contents for information on printing additional copies.)

 Troubleshooting Tip

For kids who don't want their friends seeing a checklist

If your child is concerned that other students will see the Locker Checklist form, recommend that your child make a personal list from some card stock. Suggest that your child decorate the list, and make it as small as possible. If it starts to work, remember to praise your child for using the list and getting the right items home.

 Troubleshooting Tip

Staying focused amid hallway craziness

The time between classes can be noisy and distracting. That may make it hard for your child to use a locker checklist. However, the distracting and noisy nature of the hallway may actually be the exact reason a checklist could be helpful. Consider some pretend practice at home. You and your child will probably find that using the checklist makes packing up go more quickly and keeps your child focused enough to be successful.

THE ROUTINE

Every time your child visits her locker, the first thing she should do is look at her locker checklist. Just as with the backpack checklist, she should go through each item and be sure it is packed in her bag before the locker is closed.

PRACTICE

After you have created the locker checklist at home with your child, practice using it a few times by creating simulations based on the actual times your child uses his locker. A bookshelf or tabletop at home can serve as his stand-in locker. Ask your child how long he typically has to make exchanges at his locker, and try to be faithful to these time limits in your simulations. Be sure to include a couple of practices for each of the different times of day during which your child uses his locker.

REWARDING CHECKLIST USE

As your child will be using the locker checklist exclusively at school, rewarding her for its proper use is difficult. Instead, you can reward her for the end goal of bringing home all needed items from her locker, including books and anything else that should be transferred home from school (accordion file, coat, lunch, etc.).

Locker Checklist

MORNING	
Classes	**Things to pack for class**

AFTERNOON	
Classes	**Things to pack for class**

END OF DAY
Things to pack for home

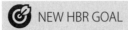 NEW HBR GOAL

Arrives home with all necessary books, supplies, and personal items from locker.

Take a Breath!

Once you have completed the Mastery Worksheet for this chapter on the facing page, you are halfway through the OST program. This is a great time to sit down with your child, pull out your two completed Mastery Worksheets, and reflect on your progress thus far. If you have made it to this point, it means both of you have done a great deal of hard work. Go ahead and retire the Go-Ahead-Lose-It Glitch in any ceremony you may have established after you completed Chapter 7. It's also not a bad time for a mini-celebration—something fun you and your child can do together to recognize your accomplishments to date.

Mastery Worksheet
Chapter 8 Goals for the Home Behavior Record

Goal	Mastery criterion	Mastered?
Has all papers filed in correct sections of accordion file, with no loose papers in backpack.	Two weeks of perfect filing.	
Receives teacher point for filing all papers correctly during class.	Two weeks of getting teacher point every day.	
Uses backpack checklist when packing backpack at night.	One week of using backpack checklist every night; then modify to new goal below.	
Uses backpack checklist when packing backpack at night, and puts all backpack items in designated containers and compartments.	One week of using backpack checklist plus containers and compartments.	
Receives teacher point for having all necessary papers and supplies in class.	Two weeks of getting teacher point every day.	
Practices "Weed It Out" with 10 sample papers.	One week of practicing "Weed It Out" each night.	
Arrives home with all necessary books, supplies, and personal items from locker.	Two weeks of arriving home with all items.	

9

Time Management
for Schoolwork

Skills taught in this chapter	Tools and routines introduced
Developing a sense of time	Lesson in understanding time Stopwatch practice
Planning homework time in the afternoon	Personal Calendar Afternoon Schedule
Avoiding distractions during homework	"Ready to Go"

Glitch we are battling:
Time Bandit

What it says: **"You can worry about your homework later. There are more fun things to do now."**

Key strategy: **Plan your time, and stick to the plan.**

By now, we hope, your child is doing pretty well in terms of knowing what homework she has to complete and having the materials she needs to complete it. Now the homework just needs to get done. This is where time management comes into play. The Time Bandit is a particularly difficult Glitch to manage, because there will always be something more enjoyable to do than homework. Our plan of attack is fourfold:

126

1. Emphasize to your child that time management is really about finding ways *to have more fun:* "If you make a clear plan for your time that includes space to relax and enjoy yourself, then that free time can truly be stress-free, because you know that there is nothing else you are supposed to be doing."

2. Help your child develop a better sense of the passage of time. For some younger children, who aren't yet able to tell time well, we start with giving them this skill. Then, for all students, we move on to methods to gain a more realistic understanding of time.

3. Help your child use this new understanding to make a schedule for each afternoon and practice, practice, practice until he is able to stick to this schedule.

4. Identify and eliminate distractions that extend homework time and thus keep your child from being able to do what she'd really like to be doing.

Developing a Sense of Time

Problems with Time Perception

Very often, children who struggle with organization also have difficulty with time perception. This may show itself when your child assures you that he can wait to do his science assignment because it "will only take five minutes," but it ends up keeping him up all night. Conversely, your child may push off facing an English assignment because it feels like it will take hours, but when he finally brings himself to sit down and start, he is able to finish in a half hour. Without an adequate sense of time, your child will have difficulty making use of tools to manage his time effectively.

ENHANCING SUCCESS

If you are like most parents, when you've thought about your child's issues with time perception, you've mostly thought about her sense that things will take less time than they really do. But the opposite misperception—that a task will take much more time than it really will—is important to recognize. It is often this opposite perception problem that leads to procrastination. As you work through the material on time management, look for opportunities to point out to your child that she is even faster and more efficient than she thought.

Our Time-Tested Solution: Lesson in Understanding Time

This lesson is specifically for younger children who have not yet learned to tell time. As the remaining skills in this chapter all rest on being able to read a clock, it is important to establish this skill first. If your child is already telling time well, feel free to skip to the next skill.

Here is a basic lesson plan for teaching your child how to tell time and calculate the passage of time. Find a time when you and your child are able to dedicate about 20 minutes to go over this lesson. Before you start, you will need an analog clock (a toy clock with movable hands or a plastic "Will return at . . . " clock will work as well), and either a digital clock or a sheet of digital clock times like the one provided below. Then go through the following steps:

1. *Teach how the hour hand works on an analog clock.* Show how the small hand moves around the clock and points to each of the 12 hours. Move the small hand one by one through each number on the clock, and explain what hour each number represents ("When the small hand is on the 1, it is 1 o'clock . . . "). Then move the small hand to five or six different hours and have your child tell you what time it is.

2. *Teach how the minute hand works.* Explain that there are 60 minutes in an hour. When 1 minute passes, it is 1 minute past the hour, and when 5 minutes pass, it is 5 minutes past the hour. Show how the same numbers that represent the 12 hours of the day also indicate 5-minute segments past the hour. Explain that counting by fives will tell how many minutes past the hour are represented by each of the numbers on the clock. Ask your child to count by 5 up to 60 minutes. Then show how the numbers represent 5 minutes, 10 minutes, and so on, past the hour. Move the minute hand around the clock and tell your child how many minutes past the hour it is at each number. Then, without moving the hour hand, select five or six times within the hour and have your child tell you what time it is.

3. *Teach how to read the hour and minute hands together.* Show five different times on the clock and explain how the time is told for these examples. (Here's an example for 1:15: "For this time, the hour hand is on the 1, and the minute hand is on the 3. The hour is 1; the minute hand is [counting out loud while pointing to 1, 2, and 3] 5, 10, 15 minutes after the hour. So it shows 15 minutes after 1, or 1:15.")

4. *Teach how a digital clock is read.* Show your child the numbers that represent the hours and the minutes. Explain how these numbers correspond

to the hours and minutes represented on an analog clock. Have her practice reading digital clock times, either on an actual digital clock or on a sheet of digital times like the one below.

3:15	6:42	9:41	11:44	5:09
1:04	6:27	5:55	5:20	12:45
7:10	4:45	10:30	12:20	3:59
2:15	8:00	9:22	5:01	7:30
11:19	3:46	1:11	2:19	10:27
3:03	6:00	12:17	4:32	6:49

Once your child is able to read both an analog and a digital clock, you can use this foundation to move on to a critical skill for managing time: developing a good sense of how long things take.

Our Time-Tested Solution: Stopwatch Practice

Stopwatch practice is a fun and effective way to help your child begin to establish a clearer sense of time. To do this practice, your child will need an inexpensive stopwatch. (If your child has a smartphone, you can also use the preinstalled stopwatch function or download a stopwatch app.) Start by sitting down with your child and explaining that you are going to spend some time over the next few days sharpening her sense of how long things take. Let her know that this is a tricky skill—even adults struggle with it—and that if she can master it, she will have a really powerful tool to help her get things done efficiently.

Then choose a task from the list below, and ask your child to write down how long he thinks it will take to complete. Have him time himself completing the task and see how close he is to his estimate. Continue with the rest of the tasks on the list. Don't be concerned if your child's estimates are wildly inaccurate at this point, because seeing that things often take more or less time than we think they will is actually an important lesson. Be sure to keep this fun and be encouraging. Let your child know that most people are less than perfect at time estimation in the beginning, and cheer when your child makes a (fairly) accurate prediction.

Tasks for Stopwatch Practice

- Blink.
- Walk across the room.
- Write out an assignment list.
- Throw a ball up and down ten times.
- Read one page in a book or magazine.
- File a paper in the accordion file.

(If you are having fun, by all means make up your own tasks and keep going!)

PRACTICE

Following this lesson, ask your child to keep the stopwatch practice going over the next week. Give your child a copy of the Activities for Stopwatch Practice form on the facing page (see the end of the Contents for information on printing copies of this form), listing various activities for your child to practice time estimation. You and your child can each choose a few activities from the form, and you can both also make up your own. For your choices, focus on activities that tend to be a struggle for your child to complete in a timely manner, or that your child complains take too much time out of his day. Ask him to time his morning routine, for example, if he is constantly at risk of missing the bus. Or ask him to time feeding the dog, if he often grumbles that he doesn't have time for this chore. Be sure, though, to stay as nonjudgmental as possible when reflecting on these time estimates: A response of "Hmm. What do you think about that?" will get you much farther than an "I told you so."

CONSTRUCTIVE CONVERSATIONS

Parent: So how long did you estimate that getting dressed and eating breakfast were going to take?

Child: Ten minutes.

Parent: How'd you actually do?

Child: It took me 25 minutes, but only because I couldn't find my red shirt today. Usually I'd be quicker.

Activities for Stopwatch Practice

Activity	Estimated time	Actual time
Turn on a computer (timed from when you press the power button to when the "Welcome" screen shows up).		
Print a page on a computer printer.		
Read a page in a novel.		
Read a page from a textbook.		
Travel to school.		
Travel home from school.		
Make a sandwich.		
Take a shower.		
Put on socks.		
Run around the park/block.		
Write three handwritten sentences.		
Complete a math worksheet.		
Get ready for school.		
Eat breakfast before school.		
Other:		
Other:		
Other:		
Other:		
Other:		

Parent: *(Tactfully refraining from mentioning that the child can't find the clothes he wants nearly every day)* Ah, so today was a little slower than it would normally be. Let's try timing again tomorrow morning. What's your new estimate going to be for a normal day?

Child: Maybe 15 or 20 minutes.

Parent: OK, we'll test that one tomorrow.

REWARDING STOPWATCH PRACTICE

For the week that your child is practicing with the stopwatch, you can award her a point on her Home Behavior Record (HBR) for practice completion. Give your child a point for completing two time estimation activities (one parent-chosen, one child-chosen) each day and briefly reflecting with you about it afterward:

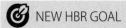 NEW HBR GOAL

Completes daily stopwatch practice.

Planning Homework Time in the Afternoon

Problems with Planning Homework Time

Once your child has begun to develop a stronger sense of the passage of time, you are ready to use this skill to help your child plan homework time more effectively. Planning for homework can be a particularly dreaded task for children who struggle with organizational skills. For some children, the thought of all the work they have to complete is so overwhelming that they won't let themselves think about it until late at night, when panic begins to set in. Other children convince themselves that they have made a mental plan of when they will get their work done, only to find that their social studies assignment took three times longer than expected, they forgot about a science quiz, and they neglected to allow time for violin practice. An effective and consistent routine for planning homework each evening can make a world of difference in your child's daily stress levels—and, by releasing you from your role of nagger-in-chief, can do a lot toward restoring your family's harmony.

Our Time-Tested Solution: The Personal Calendar

Establishing an effective routine for planning homework starts with the Personal Calendar. This is a small card listing each day of the week that serves as a reminder for any regularly scheduled activities your child should consider when planning her afternoon. You can make your own Personal Calendar by using the template on the following page (see the end of the Contents for information on printing more copies of the template) and attach it to your planner. Next to each day of the week, your child should list any regularly scheduled commitments that fall on that day of the week, along with their start and end times. A sample filled-in calendar is also shown on the following page, below the template. Having a Personal Calendar visible gives your child a clear reminder of all of the time constraints she should consider when planning her time for homework completion.

Our Time-Tested Solution: The Afternoon Schedule

Once the Personal Calendar is put together, your child is ready to begin using the Afternoon Schedule, the tool at the heart of afternoon planning. In our planner, this appears as a sidebar on the right-hand side of the Daily Assignment Record (DAR) in Chapter 7. (If you are using a different planner, you can print out copies of the Afternoon Schedule on page 135; see the end of the Contents for information.) The Afternoon Schedule is a space where your child should list times from the end of school to bedtime and then fill in the homework and activities he plans to complete next to the times he plans to complete them. A sample filled-out Afternoon Schedule is also shown on page 135.

THE ROUTINE

Make an agreement with your child about when she should sit down to plan her homework time each afternoon. We recommend that this be done either as soon as your child arrives home or after a small break of a set, agreed-upon duration. If you like to give your child some time to unwind after school before homework, that's fine—but it is important to make the homework plan first, so that she knows how long she can relax and still have time left to comfortably complete all her work and anything else she would like to do.

When your child sits down to make his plan and fill out his Afternoon Schedule, he should start by reviewing the following information (page 136):

Personal Calendar

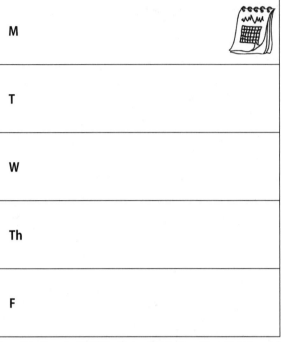

M	
T	
W	
Th	
F	

Personal Calendar : Example

M 3:30 Soccer	
T	
W 6:00 Violin	
Th 3:00 Homework help	
F	

Afternoon Schedule

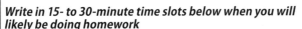

WHAT is there to do? (Check DAR & A&TC.)

HOW LONG will it take?

WHEN can I fit it in?

Write in 15- to 30-minute time slots below when you will likely be doing homework

Started HW: Early/on time/late

Finished HW: Early/on time/late

Afternoon Schedule: Example

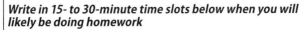

WHAT is there to do? (Check DAR & A&TC.)

HOW LONG will it take?

WHEN can I fit it in?

Write in 15- to 30-minute time slots below when you will likely be doing homework

3:30	Snack
4:00	Math worksheet
4:30	Daily reading
5:00	Break
5:30	Dinner
6:00	Study for science
6:30	Relax

Started HW: Early/on time/late

Finished HW: Early/on time/late

- The homework he has listed on his DAR for that day.

- Any long-term assignments listed on the Assignment and Test Calendar (see Chapter 7 for the calendar itself, and Chapter 10 for a full discussion of its use) that may need to be worked on that afternoon.

- Regular commitments for that day listed on the Personal Calendar.

Your child should then make a time estimate for each task and activity he has to complete, and block out time for that task/activity on the schedule. It is important that he schedule each task individually. For example, he might estimate that his social studies assignment will take 15 minutes, and then block out time from 3:45 to 4:00 to complete it. He should *not* estimate that his homework as a whole will take an hour, and then block out time from 3:30 to 4:30 that just reads "Homework." The larger task of "homework" contains too many smaller tasks, which will make it difficult for your child to estimate the time it will take to complete all of those tasks together. And if his time estimate is off, it makes it difficult for him to pinpoint where the error was, and he will not learn how to improve his planning in the future.

 ENHANCING SUCCESS

As we've noted at the beginning of the chapter, it's important for kids to know that time management doesn't just help them get their work done; it also gives them more time to have fun and relax without the weight of uncompleted work hanging over them. When your child is making her afternoon plans, encourage her to schedule some fun things as well. Ask her to think of what she would like to do in the afternoon, and have her create a schedule with time for that built in.

PRACTICE

Let your child take the lead in filling out his Afternoon Schedule. As you watch him work, you can ask him questions to understand his thought process, but try not to be overly directive. You will undoubtedly notice that your child's first plans include glaringly unrealistic aspects, but the most effective way to teach him is to let him try out his plans and then reflect on where they failed, with the understanding that making mistakes is a constructive part of the learning process. To that end, while your child is still learning how to make effective plans, have him mark down the time he *actually* completed each assignment or activity to the right of the space where it was listed. Then, in a nonjudgmental manner, review with your child at the end of the evening how his plan went, and ask him what changes he thinks he should make to create a more realistic plan the next day.

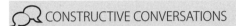 CONSTRUCTIVE CONVERSATIONS

Making the Initial Plan

Parent: OK, what should we schedule in first?

Child: My Art class assignment. It's easy, so it should take 5 minutes. My bus gets here at 3:30, so I'll do it from 3:30 to 3:35.

Parent: *(Biting tongue to keep from mentioning that the child always takes much longer than that on Art assignments, is ignoring the time it takes to get in the door from the bus stop, and never wants to start homework right away when getting home)* OK. Let's write that in. What do we need to schedule next?

Reflecting on the Plan in the Evening

Parent: How did your plan go? What time did you do your Art assignment?

Child: From 4:00 to 4:30. I forgot I would need a snack first, and it took longer than I thought it would.

Parent: Well, that's a great observation. That's really going to help you with your planning tomorrow. Let's remember that when we make our plan. You are doing great work with this—each day you are figuring out something new and important about what kind of plan works best for you!

REWARDING AFTERNOON SCHEDULE USE

Use of the Afternoon Schedule can be added to the HBR as follows:

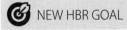 NEW HBR GOAL

Creates afternoon plan, and writes down the times assignments are actually completed, on the Afternoon Schedule.

You can award this point when you sit down with your child to review how that day's plan went. If your child is resistant to sitting down with you to reflect on the plan each evening, you can make this discussion a condition of awarding the point. It is important to note that this point (and your praise) should *not* be dependent on the accuracy of the plan. This is a learning process, and the goal is for your child to be engaged in this process in a meaningful way, not for her to develop this skill overnight.

Avoiding Distractions during Homework

Problems with Distractions

As your child works on his Afternoon Schedules, it is likely that one fact will jump out at him: He is sadly in need of more free time. As an adult who is juggling the demands of daily life, parenting, and a time-intensive (though incredibly worthwhile!) organizational skills training program, you may have less than full sympathy for your child's plight. But giving your child your support in his goal of finding more time for fun and relaxation in his day can be very productive. One way he can find more time for himself is to become an expert planner through using the methods described above. Another is to help him work more efficiently during homework time. This means taking on one of the biggest homework time problems: distraction.

 Troubleshooting Tip

Is your child taking medication for ADHD?

As we've discussed at the start of this book, ADHD is a common reason why children have organizational skills deficits. If your child has been diagnosed with ADHD and prescribed medication, talk to your child's doctor if he has ongoing problems with distractibility at school or while doing homework. Distractibility is one of the main symptoms that medication is supposed to address, so a medication review may be warranted.

Our Time-Tested Solution: "Ready to Go"

To address the problem of distractions during homework, we recommend a procedure called "Ready to Go." This procedure involves two steps:

1. *Look over your homework and gather all the supplies you will need before beginning to work.* This avoids the distraction of constantly

getting up to find needed materials (pencil, protractor, notebook, etc.).

2. *Look around your work space and put away anything that is unnecessary and could provide a potential distraction.* This can involve both storing away distracting objects (such as small toys, handheld games, and phones) and closing out or disabling distractions on the computer (such as social media).

PRACTICE

We like to practice "Ready to Go" skills in the context of a game. Come up with a few fun tasks (making a peanut butter and jelly sandwich, say, or going on a day trip). Then put the supplies for those tasks out on your child's desk or work space, and add a bunch of unrelated and potentially distracting items (small toys, knickknacks, etc.). Invite your child to the desk/work space, and present her with one of the tasks. Then see how quickly she can find all of the items she needs for that task and put away anything unnecessary.

You can do further practice with your child's actual homework. Help him look over his assignments and think through any supplies he will need. Then have him gather those supplies and rid the work space of anything distracting.

REWARDING "READY TO GO"

Once your child has the hang of it, make her responsible for getting her work space "Ready to Go" before homework each afternoon. Watch as she prepares the space, and ask questions to determine how she has decided what she needs and what should be put away. She can earn a point on the HBR for engaging in this process.

 NEW HBR GOAL

Gets work space "Ready to Go" correctly before starting homework.

Take a Breath!

As in previous weeks, be sure to check off goals your child has mastered on the Mastery Worksheet on the following page and replace them on the HBR with new behavior goals.

Once this Mastery Worksheet is completed, you and your child have now officially vanquished the Time Bandit. Three Glitches down, and now only one left to go. Have your child pencil in a little time in his schedule for the two of you to celebrate!

Mastery Worksheet
Chapter 9 Goals for the Home Behavior Record

Goal	Mastery criterion	Mastered?
Completes daily stopwatch practice.	One week of stopwatch practice.	
Creates afternoon plan, and writes down the times assignments are actually completed, on the Afternoon Schedule.	Two weeks of creating and following afternoon plan.	
Gets work space "Ready to Go" correctly before starting homework.	One week of practicing "Ready to Go."	

10

Planning for Long-Term Assignments and Tests

Skills taught in this chapter	Tools and routines introduced
Planning for long-term assignments and tests	Task-Planning Sheet Assignment and Test Calendar (for scheduling long-term assignments) The Mastermind Master Plan
Checking work to make sure it is done well, neatly, and completely	"Check It Out"

Glitch we are battling:
Go-Ahead-Don't-Plan Glitch

What it says: **"You have plenty of time. You don't need to think about your work now."**

Key strategy: **Plan ahead, and make a reasonable schedule.**

If there was a straw that broke the camel's back and led you to buy this book, most likely it involved a poorly planned-for long-term assignment or test that kept the family up all night in a haze of stress and tears. We've all lost a battle with the Go-Ahead-Don't-Plan Glitch at some point in our lives, but for children with organizational skills difficulties, procrastination is more often the rule than the exception. The thought of all the work involved in completing large assignments or preparing for important tests is often so overwhelming for children who struggle with organization that they cope by pushing it to the back of their minds until the last minute, when panic sets in. The solutions in this chapter aim to prevent the last-minute rush and help ease the pressure on your child.

If your child is too young to be receiving long-term assignments or tests, bookmark this chapter for later, and teach him the strategies presented here in time to apply them to his very first long-term assignments. Long-term planning is highly challenging for most children who struggle with organizational skills, even those who have mastered strategies to overcome other organizational challenges. But there's no point in adding tools and skills to their toolboxes that they can't use yet.

Long-Term Planning

Problems with Long-Term Planning

As discussed throughout this book, many children who struggle with organization have a cognitive style that favors short-term rewards over long-term rewards. This style underlies many of the problems these children have with organizational tasks. For your child, for example, the short-term reward of stuffing a paper in her bag and getting to leave class a few seconds earlier may trump the long-term reward of being able to locate the paper when she needs it and the longer-term reward of getting a good grade on her assignment. As you can imagine, this cognitive style creates even more challenges when children must work on a long-term assignment; in this case, the academic rewards are days or even weeks in the future, and the short-term temptations are numerous. This tendency to choose short-term over long-term rewards, coupled with confusion about how to tackle a larger assignment or test, gives the Go-Ahead-Don't-Plan Glitch plenty of room to wreak havoc.

Our Time-Tested Solution: The Task-Planning Sheet

The Task-Planning Sheet—one of the planner tools you've included when you've put together your child's planner as described in Chapter 7—is a simple form we have developed to help students break large assignments or tests down into manageable steps. This form is provided on page 144 (see the end of the Contents for information on downloading and printing extra copies of the form for your child's planner). Here are the key features:

1. The first column—"What steps need to be taken?"—provides a space for your child to list each of the steps he will need to complete for the assignment. These should be broken down to a level where each step can be completed in one sitting. Each step should also be *concrete and specific:* Your child should know exactly what he needs to do and what it means for that step to be complete. "Study Chapter 12," for example, is too vague. "Read through Chapter 12 once, and make a list of all key terms" is a better option.

2. The second column—"What stuff do I need?"—is a prompt for your child to consider what supplies she will need to complete each step. This ensures that she doesn't plan to work on a step on a given afternoon, only to discover that she doesn't have the materials she needs. Also, filling out the "What stuff . . . ?" column may help your child think of additional steps she needs to add to the first column. Let's say your child is planning for a science fair project and writes down this step: "Paste pictures onto poster board for display." In the "What stuff . . . ?" column for this step, she may write: "Pictures, scissors, glue, poster board." She may then realize that she needs to buy poster board. "Buy poster board" can be added as another step in the first column.

3. The final column—"How long will each step take?"—gives your child a space to put his time estimation skills to use in figuring out the amount of time he will need to set aside for each step. As with the previous exercises in time estimation (see Chapter 9), the guesses here are likely to be inaccurate at first. Remember to frame this as part of a learning process. When things take a longer or shorter time than expected, help your child take note, so that he can make more accurate predictions the next time.

As you may imagine, the next step is to use all of this information to schedule times to complete the long-term assignment or prepare for the big test. We like to stop here, though, and take some time for children to practice and strengthen their use of these steps before moving on to scheduling. While the process of long-term planning as a whole may seem simple, it involves a number of skills that are often particularly challenging to students who struggle with organization. Taking your time with this process is the best path to success.

Task-Planning Sheet

What project/test?			What project/test?		
What steps need to be taken?	What stuff do I need?	How long will each step take?	What steps need to be taken?	What stuff do I need?	How long will each step take?

THE ROUTINE

On the day a new long-term assignment or test is assigned, your child should sit down and break it down on a copy of the Task-Planning Sheet. While your child is developing this skill, sitting with her as she goes through the routine is helpful. Let her take the lead, but chime in with questions if you notice a missing step or a time estimate that may need rethinking.

 Troubleshooting Tip

When the Task-Planning Sheet feels like overkill

Once your child has become skilled at the long-term planning process, going through these steps for each assignment and test may feel like busywork. At that point, your child can graduate to a more simplified routine. He will likely be able to complete the steps listed on the Task-Planning Sheet mentally and skip directly to scheduling the steps on the Assignment and Test Calendar, as described below.

PRACTICE

For the first week that this skill is introduced, your child should be completing a copy of the Task-Planning Sheet for at least one task each day. Ideally, these tasks will be actual assignments or tests your child receives. You can dip into the backlog of any projects your child was given previously and is (or should be!) currently working on, and you should certainly use any new assignments your child is given. Still, it is unlikely that you will have enough material to allow for a new plan each day. In the absence of real assignments or tests, you can have your child plan for non-school-related activities (an upcoming trip, a social activity with friends), or you can make up assignments for your child to plan.

Blank copies of the Task-Planning Sheet can be stored in the left-hand pocket of your child's planner, if you are using a folder for the planner (see the book's Appendix; the online supplementary appendix gives instructions for where to place these copies if you are having a planner put together at a copy shop). Once a project is completed, there's no need to hang on to the used Task-Planning Sheets; they can be discarded.

REWARDING TASK PLANNING

Your child can receive a point on the Home Behavior Record (HBR) for completing a copy of the Task-Planning Sheet each afternoon:

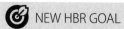 NEW HBR GOAL

Completes one copy of the Task-Planning Sheet.

After a week of practice with this form, your child should be ready to move on to the last step in this process: committing time to complete each step of his plan.

Our Time-Tested Solution: The Assignment and Test Calendar

With a set of clearly delineated steps for our assignment in hand, we turn back to a tool we've first introduced in Chapter 7: the Assignment and Test Calendar. Now, in addition to the final due dates for assignments and tests, you and your child will be using the calendar to list each step needed to complete the assignment on the day your child plans to complete it.

Have your child sit down with her Assignment and Test Calendar and a completed copy of the Task-Planning Sheet in front of her. Then have her select a date for each of the steps she has listed, and write the step on the date she has chosen to work on it. Once again, let her take the lead, but prompt her with questions to consider.

 ENHANCING SUCCESS

Be sure to have your child enter the tasks into the Assignment and Test Calendar in pencil. As your child works through the process, she may discover that she needs to begin work earlier than she anticipated, or to reconsider how much she needs to get done on a given day.

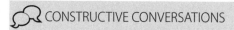 CONSTRUCTIVE CONVERSATIONS

Parent: All right. Your biography is due Friday, and today is Monday. When do you want to do your first step?

Child: I think I'll start tomorrow. I'll put down the first one: "Find sources online."

Parent: OK, what's next?

Child: I'll put "Read and take notes on sources" for Wednesday. Oh, but then I only have Thursday left for my last three steps. Maybe I will also put "Write first draft" on Wednesday.

Parent: OK. But remember, you also have a friend coming over on Wednesday. Do you think you'll have time?

Child: Maybe not. Maybe I should move my first step to today.

Parent: Great idea. Let's erase and start again.

THE ROUTINE

Now, when your child plans for her long-term assignments or tests, she should add each step to the Assignment and Test Calendar as the last part of the process. In time, the planning will probably be done mentally as mentioned above, and the child can just enter the tasks on the calendar after thinking through the assignment.

PRACTICE

Sitting with your child, helping him make plans for his assignments, and helping him schedule them into his Assignment and Test Calendar provide the most effective practice for learning to plan effectively. However, a similar problem as with the Task-Planning Sheet is that most students do not receive enough long-term work to provide material for a week's worth of practice with the Assignment and Test Calendar. Again, you can substitute planning for social activities or personal goals, or you can create hypothetical assignments. Aim to practice making one plan each day for the next week.

REWARDING PLANNING WITH THE ASSIGNMENT AND TEST CALENDAR

You can now alter the point your child has been receiving for filling out copies of the Task-Planning Sheet, to reward her instead for using the Assignment and Test Calendar to follow through on long-term plans she has created.

Troubleshooting Tip

What if your child gets behind right away?

If your child fails to complete his scheduled work for one day, he can fall behind and have trouble earning his point on subsequent days. If this happens, help him create an adjusted plan to account for the work he needs to make up. If he follows this adjusted plan in the following days, he should still receive his point on those days.

 NEW HBR GOAL

Completes long-term assignment/test work scheduled for today, listed on the Assignment and Test Calendar.

By now your child has amassed a strong set of tools for managing time and planning for work completion. The task now is to help your child develop a consistent routine, so that use of these tools becomes an ingrained part of her everyday life.

Our Time-Tested Solution: The Mastermind Master Plan

The Mastermind Master Plan is the name we give to the routine that takes all of the tools your child has learned for short- and long-term time management and integrates them. In conjunction, these tools provide the Mastermind with a considerable arsenal in its fight against the Time Bandit and the Go-Ahead-Don't Plan Glitch. It is important to allow your child some time to consolidate what he has learned, and spending a week or so rewarding use of the Mastermind Master Plan will help ensure that use of these routines becomes a well-established habit.

THE ROUTINE

Each afternoon, before starting homework, your child should sit down with his planner and create a Mastermind Master Plan. Ask him to go through the following steps:

1. First, look at your Personal Calendar. Check for any regular commitments scheduled for the day and block them out on the Afternoon Schedule.

2. Next, check the Daily Assignment Record (DAR) for any new long-term assignments or tests given that day. Write the due date(s) on the Assignment and Test Calendar. Then use the steps on the Task-Planning Sheet to break things down (either on paper or mentally). Write the steps on the days of the Assignment and Test Calendar you plan to complete them.

3. Look at the assignments listed on today's DAR, as well as any steps from long-term assignments scheduled for today on the Assignment and Test Calendar. Block out time for each on the Afternoon Schedule.

REWARDING USE OF THE MASTERMIND MASTER PLAN

The components of the Mastermind Master Plan (long-term assignment/ test planning and use of the Afternoon Schedule) have either already appeared in goals on your child's HBR or are currently included among these goals. These are often some of the most difficult skills to acquire, so for most children, it makes sense to keep these as separate goals on the HBR. If, however, your child has reached a point where these routines are well ingrained, you can trade them for a single goal of using the Mastermind Master Plan each afternoon.

 NEW HBR GOAL (OPTIONAL)

Uses the Mastermind Master Plan.

Checking Work

If you, your child, or both of you are starting to feel overwhelmed with all of these new routines and tools, we have some good news: You have now reached the very last skill we teach in our program. If, by any chance, your eyes are glazing over as you are reading this, and you are thinking it might not be such a big deal to skip this last skill, then you are in a good position to empathize with the very problem this routine addresses. Many students who struggle with organization are so relieved to have answered the last question on their very last homework assignment for the evening that they find it all too tempting to skip what should be the last step of homework: checking everything to make sure it is done neatly, accurately, and completely.

Our Time-Tested Solution: "Check It Out"

"Check It Out" simply means taking the time to go over work to be sure that there are no errors, the instructions have been followed, the work is neat, and it is completely finished. Talk to your child about what steps she should be taking to check her assignments. Some examples for specific types of homework are provided in the box on the facing page. The key is making this process concrete, with clear indications of exactly what your child should be looking out for. Emphasize to your child that careless errors are the Glitches' last opportunity to get her in trouble. If she is able to resist the urge to skip the step of checking things, she will have taken the very last measure necessary to defeat the Glitches once and for all.

THE ROUTINE

At the end of each assignment, your child should cast a critical eye over what he has done, to be sure the work is done well and is neat and complete. As he is first learning this skill, it can be helpful for you to sit with him and have him go through the process out loud.

PRACTICE

In addition to helping your child as she checks her actual homework, you can simulate some assignments and have her see how many errors she can catch. On page 152 is a box containing a sample assignment with five errors that your child can try to find. (These are the errors: no name on homework paper; "blissful" is not in alphabetical order; "excited" is spelled incorrectly; there are only 11 words [there is no item 5]; and no word is starred.) You can also invite your child to find errors in your work—mistakes you made on a shopping list, say, or in filling out a form.

REWARDING "CHECK IT OUT"

As your child is practicing "Check It Out," you can give him a point for going through the process out loud for one of his assignments each day.

 NEW HBR GOAL

Practices "Check It Out."

How to "Check It Out" For . . .

. . . AN ESSAY

- Did I put in my name?
- Did I follow all the instructions?
- Will my teacher be able to read my handwriting?
- Did I spell everything correctly?
- Is my grammar correct?

. . . A SET OF MATH PROBLEMS

- Did I put in my name?
- Did I follow all the instructions?
- Did I do all the problems I was supposed to?
- Did I double-check my calculations?
- Did I show my work when I was supposed to?

. . . A SET OF TEXTBOOK QUESTIONS

- Did I put in my name?
- Did I follow all the instructions?
- Did I answer all the questions I was supposed to?
- Did I check all my answers against the book?
- Will my teacher be able to read my handwriting?
- Did I spell everything correctly?

. . . A WORKSHEET

- Did I put in my name?
- Did I follow all the instructions?
- Did I answer all of the questions?
- Will my teacher be able to read my handwriting?
- Did I spell everything correctly?

. . . A JOURNAL ENTRY

- Did I follow all the instructions?
- Will my teacher be able to read my handwriting?
- Did I spell everything correctly?
- Is my grammar correct?

Sample Assignment

Instructions: Check this student's completed homework. See if you can find five errors.

VOCABULARY HOMEWORK

Name: _____

Please list 12 different words that mean "happy" in alphabetical order. Be sure they are spelled correctly. When you are done, put a star next to your favorite word.

1. Cheerful
2. Content
3. Blissful
4. Exscited
6. Glad
7. Gleeful
8. Jolly
9. Joyful
10. Optimistic
11. Pleased
12. Smiling

Congratulations: You've Both Graduated!

Be sure to check off the new HBR goals on the Mastery Worksheet on the facing page as your child meets the mastery criteria. And once this last Mastery Worksheet is completed, you and your child have officially graduated! Your child is an organizational Mastermind, and you are an expert-level parent coach!

Now, if you are anything like most parents in our program, you've just read those last two sentences with some small misgivings. Your child still may not have gotten the hang of some skills and may have had a couple of setbacks on skills that she seemed to have mastered. *This is OK.* These skills take time to become habits, and if you were to chart the progress of even our most shining success stories, it could never be plotted as a straight line upward. Success always comes in peaks and valleys, with a general trend toward improvement. It is important for both you and your child to know that the Glitches never completely leave. They will always creep back in to see if they have any room to get back to their old tricks. The difference between a student who stays organized and one who falls back into old habits is not that the successful student never makes any mistakes. The difference is that when the Glitches return, the successful student recognizes the problem, checks which routines may have been slipping, and gets to work on reestablishing them.

That being said, even if you and your child are not yet where you would like to be, there is still cause for celebration. You have both done a great deal of work and built up an important skill set. Take some time to reflect on where your child was when you first embarked on the program and where he is now. Be sure he is aware of all of the progress you have seen. And then find a fun way to celebrate together!

Mastery Worksheet
Chapter 10 Goals for the Home Behavior Record

Goal	Mastery criterion	Mastered?
Completes one copy of the Task-Planning Sheet.	One week of completing a sheet daily.	
Completes long-term assignment/test work scheduled for today, using the Assignment and Test Calendar.	Two weeks of perfect completion.	
Uses the Mastermind Master Plan.	One to two weeks of using the plan daily.	
Practices "Check It Out."	One week of practice each day.	

Part IV

Putting the Last Pieces in Place

If your child has difficulty with organization, time management, and planning (OTMP) skills for school-related tasks, you've probably noticed issues in the same areas at home. A child who forgets about assignments is also likely to have issues remembering the schedule for her Little League softball game or the household chores she is supposed to complete each week. If your child loses papers and books at school, you probably hear the following refrain at home more often than you can count: "Where's my [insert name of precious toy/doll/electronic device]??" In this part of the book, we discuss classic scenarios where the Glitches interfere in your child's daily life outside the school setting, and share tips and tricks that will help your child keep the Mastermind in control at all times.

Your personal style and level of organization are important to consider as you read through the chapters in this section. When children are very young, they rely on parents to control their daily schedule, set up a system for organizing toys and other items, keep track of when they need to be where, and plan ahead. As you have probably observed among your friends and family members, not every parent accomplishes these tasks in the same way. You've all met the parent (and perhaps you are this parent) whose phone calendar contains the dates and times for every doctor's appointment, playdate, school event, holiday, and birthday party in a three-month window. This parent drops the child off at school precisely on time every morning; has a perfectly wrapped gift ready three days before each birthday party; and arrives at the park with a bag packed with hand wipes, snacks, drinks, and Band-Aids. Not everyone can achieve this "executive assistant" level of organized parenting. Most of us fall along a continuum that spreads away from this pinnacle point, ranging from "mostly getting by" to "barely on top of things" to "always a step behind."

Whether you are an executive assistant parent or one of the latter types, you can benefit from reading Chapter 11, the first chapter in Part IV. For those of you who are executive assistant parents, your task (and this can be quite challenging for those with a natural desire to exert control in all things) will be to start relinquishing some of the control over organizational tasks to your children, with step-by-step guidance. For those of you who struggle to stay on top of after-school activities, mountains of toys, and endless events, the tools that we recommend in the following chapters will help you and your children work together so that you both feel more on top of daily demands.

For each organizational task required in the home setting, we introduce our time-tested solutions, which are based on the same principles that inspired the development of the tips and tricks presented in Part III. We'll highlight key features of each tool or routine, walk you through the establishment of a routine that incorporates that tool/routine, and indicate how you can motivate use of the tool/routine by using the "prompt–praise–monitor–reward" sequence introduced in Part II. Depending on your child's particular needs, you may choose to focus on prompting and rewarding the school-related organized behaviors in Part III before moving on to address the home-related behaviors covered in this section. Alternatively, you may integrate school- and home-related organizational tasks in your Home Behavior Record (HBR), if both types are of equal concern and impact as indicated by your child's OTMP Inventory in Chapter 3. In either case, keep in mind that for a new behavior to be integrated into your child's daily routine, you will need to provide clear, frequent reminders, labeled praise, and rewards as the behavior is being learned.

If you're integrating home-related organizational tasks into your work on school-related problems, keep in mind that you may have to refer to the appropriate skill instructions in Part III to work on a particular home problem. Chapter 11 also includes directions to the chapters where you'll find those instructions.

Finally, we want to emphasize an important principle to keep in mind as you teach your child to take more responsibility for managing personal items, schedules, and responsibilities: Forget about your preconceived notions regarding what your child *should* or *should not* be able to do. You might think that your seven-year-old child *should* be able to take a shower, brush her teeth, and get into bed without prompts or help from you, because her older sister performed these tasks without any difficulty at that age. Alternatively, you might not believe that your nine-year-old child can independently pack a bag for swim practice without forgetting his goggles, so you insist on packing the bag for him.

It is natural to make these kinds of assumptions. After all, most of us parent by using our intuition, making predictions about what will or will not work based on our past experience or observations of other parents and children. However, we strongly suggest that instead of focusing on the "shoulds," you focus on the "cans." What *can* your child already do, and how might that change if you give her the opportunity to do more by providing just a little support? If your child already packs the swim bag with 90% of what he needs, maybe a simple checklist will ensure that he is 100% accurate every time. If your child can easily get into pajamas and brush her teeth in five minutes, but tends to daydream in the shower, can you set a timer for a five- minute shower and help her complete her entire bedtime routine more efficiently? As you read Chapter 11, pay attention to what your child is already able to do, and think about how you can shift your expectations and routines a bit so that your child is capable of performing even more organizational tasks with ease.

Once you have read Chapter 11, you should be ready to integrate all of the tips and tricks you have learned to help your child become more organized in school and at home . . . but just in case, we've outlined what an "organized day" looks like in Chapter 12. We also provide some ideas for keeping your child motivated to use organizational tools and routines, after the initial excitement of the points-and-rewards system wears off. You probably do not plan to reward your child with rewards for packing her backpack every day for the rest of her school career—and you shouldn't! At the end of Chapter 12, we teach you how to fade out prompts and thin out your reward system, slowly and in a way that keeps your child invested in staying organized.

Finally, in Chapter 13, we discuss what to do if you've tried the steps in the Organizational Skills Training (OST) program but still feel that your child is not making progress. If that is the case, you may need to seek out professional assistance—and we've laid out some ideas to consider and steps to take, so that your child can get the necessary support to move forward.

11

Managing the Glitches
at Home

In Part III we've described how the Glitches—those metaphorical creatures in your child's brain that discourage organized actions—interfere with your child's ability to keep track of assignments and materials, manage time effectively, and plan ahead for school-related tasks. While the Glitches are best known for their destructive impact at school and with regard to school-related tasks, they can also wreak havoc at home. If your child has organizational difficulties, it is likely that there are issues at home with managing toys and other personal items, completing daily routines, and approaching personal tasks with appropriate planning. The tips that we provide below will help you and your child get the Glitches under control at home.

Managing "Stuff" at Home

Glitch we are battling:
Go-Ahead-Lose-It Glitch

What it says: **"Hurry up; we have to do something else. Just drop that toy over there, and you can put it away later."**

Key strategy: **Having a place for everything, and putting everything back in its place as soon as you are finished with it.**

The strategies in this section are directly related to steps introduced in Chapter 8 for managing papers and other items in your child's school bag. Please read Chapter 8 first for an orientation to approaches for materials management.

If your home is anything like our homes, the amount of "stuff" that your child owns seems to multiply on a daily basis. The toys, games, and electronic devices your child receives for birthdays and holidays; equipment for sports and other hobbies; goody bags from birthday parties; and prizes from the dentist's office all flow into your home at a steady pace that threatens to bury every available surface. It should not surprise you, then, when your child misplaces items. When the Go-Ahead-Lose-It Glitch targets one of your child's "favorite" items, though, it is not fun for anyone involved. Let's review some basic tips that can help you teach your child how to keep the Mastermind in control of toys and other important items. Using these tips may result in two intended side effects—namely, a cleaner room and a reduced need to nag your child to clean his room every day.

Our Time-Tested Solution: Storage Containers

Your child will need a bit of help from you to set up an organized environment for storing toys and other personal items. First, you will want to assess how your child's things are currently organized. Are all your child's things stored in one location or in several places throughout the house? Do you have enough drawers, storage boxes, baskets, and other containers to hold your child's things, or are many items loose on counters, desks, or floors? Consider how the current situation can be improved, keeping in mind our general advice to keep it simple. If possible, your child's things should all be in one room (preferably her own bedroom, or a playroom if you prefer to keep the bedroom free of distracting items, as discussed in Chapter 8) and stored in clearly defined storage containers/drawers or on specified shelves. You may need to rethink your storage plan or purchase additional storage containers after you've taken inventory of what things your child has and will actually be keeping (see below).

🏆 ENHANCING SUCCESS

You may need to test different options to see what works best for you and your child. But in the same way you probably store similar items together (pots and pans in certain kitchen cabinets and dishes in others, towels on certain shelves in your linen closet, etc.), your child will stay more organized at home if you identify categories of items that can each be stored in their own containers. For example, if your child plays with a set of small dolls and props together, store those items all in one box so that they can be easily cleaned up when playtime is over. Set aside a special drawer for electronic devices and their associated chargers, cables, and attachments. Avoid placing many different kinds of items in large storage containers; it's easy for smaller items to get lost in a large box or basket, and it will be more difficult for your child to find specific items if everything is thrown into one large box. If he can't easily find what he wants, he's not likely to be motivated to return it to the box. (Remember, the point of using storage containers isn't just to keep your home neat; it's to teach your child that he can get organized and that being organized has rewards.) Whenever possible, label storage containers so that your child knows where to store each item, or use clear containers so your child can easily see the contents.

Before setting up a new storage plan, you should take a critical inventory of the "stuff" that your child owns. Use a modified version of the "Weed It Out" procedure explained in Chapter 8 to help your child take stock of her things. You may want to set aside a few hours to conduct this initial inventory, depending on how many things your child has. Go around the house and examine each item that your child owns, carrying three boxes or large bags labeled "Keep," "Give away," and "Garbage." Help your child look at each item with a critical eye, and encourage her to think about how often she has used it in the past three months. If an item is never or almost never used, your child should give it away (if it's in good condition) or throw it in the garbage (if it's no longer usable). If your child does use it, put it in the "Keep" box.

Once you've decided which items to keep, work with your child to determine where each thing or set of things should be stored. It's important to involve your child so he'll use the system created. Involving your child in making the decisions will also teach him how to set up a storage system and how to approach organization in a thoughtful way. Help your child consider questions such as these:

"Where do I usually use these art supplies, and where should I store them?"

"Will I be able to find this toy if I keep it in this box?"

"Which toys should I store in an easily accessible place, because I use them a lot? And which should I store in a closet, because I don't use them as much?"

Of course, as you use whatever system you set up, you or your child may notice flaws and can shift things around.

THE ROUTINE

The routine for managing toys and personal items is similar to that for managing items in a backpack, using containers and compartments (see Chapter 8). First, your child needs to remember where each item is stored. You can help by labeling storage containers or selecting clear containers, as suggested above. The most important task, though, will be to help your child develop the habit of putting every item back in its place immediately after using it. Remind your child that otherwise, the Go-Ahead-Lose-It Glitch will happily suggest that the child simply leave the item in any place that is most convenient at the time, increasing the chances that the item will be lost or misplaced. Talk together about the ways the Glitch might try to trap your child into losing different items, and brainstorm ways to put the Glitch in its place.

CONSTRUCTIVE CONVERSATIONS

Parent: Can you think of some things that you often have trouble finding in the house?

Child: I guess sometimes I have trouble finding my softball mitt—usually right before I need it for practice!

Parent: Yup, and I'll bet the Go-Ahead-Lose-It Glitch is thrilled when you get in trouble with the coach for being late because it took you 10 minutes to find your mitt. Let's think about why the Glitch has such an easy time making you lose your mitt. Where do you usually keep it?

Child: Well, it depends. Sometimes I find it in the backyard, sometimes it's in the garage, sometimes it's in the softball bag with the bats and stuff, and sometimes it's in my room. One time I even found it under the living room couch!

Parent: So it sounds like you don't have one set place where you put your mitt back every time you finish using it. Let's think about one place that would make the most sense, and then practice putting it there every single time you finish using it. That way, the Glitch won't be able to get you in trouble. What would be the easiest place for you to remember to put your mitt after you're done with it?

Child: Probably in my softball bag—that way, it would always be there when I need it for practice. But maybe we can move the bag to the playroom, so I can drop it in there when I come in from outside, instead of having to go to the garage to find it.

Parent: Great idea! That will make it easier for you to remember to always put it back after you're done using it.

PRACTICE

Help your child practice putting things away right away in selected storage containers by going through some practice runs. For example, if your child often loses track of her softball mitt (as in the example above), take her outside to play a game of catch, and then prompt her to return the mitt to the softball bag as soon as you return inside. Try to go through this routine a few times; praise her for remembering to put her special item away immediately in a set location; and award a point for using storage containers and managing her stuff.

REWARDING USE OF STORAGE CONTAINERS

Once you've set up a system for storing particular items in specific containers, you can add a goal to the Home Behavior Record (HBR) related to this organizational skill. If your child successfully stores the specified items in the proper locations, you can award a point on the HBR. Once your child becomes more adept at this skill, you can award a point for storing all personal items in their proper locations.

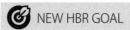 NEW HBR GOAL

Puts specified personal items in designated storage containers/locations.

Packing and Managing Bags: The Activity Bag Checklist

Glitch we are battling:
Go-Ahead-Lose-It Glitch

What it says: **"You don't need to pack your bag for practice; your mom will make sure you have everything you need."**

Key strategy: **Using checklists to make sure you have what you need.**

The strategies in this section are directly related to steps introduced in Chapter 8 for creating a backpack checklist. Please read Chapter 8 first for an orientation to approaches for materials management.

Once you've tackled the question of where your child's things should be stored in your home, you will want to think about how you can help your child transport things out of the house and back. In Chapter 8 we've introduced a tool, the backpack checklist, to help your child make sure that all needed items are packed in the school backpack. You can help your child make similar checklists for other bags. First, think about activities that require the packing of a bag with special items—for example, sleepovers, long weekends at a grandparent's house, a day at the pool/beach, or extracurricular activities (sports, dance, etc.). If your child spends time in different households during the week or participates in multiple extracurricular activities, helping the child think about necessary items to pack in a bag will be particularly important.

The steps to follow in creating an activity bag checklist are identical to those that we recommend in Chapter 8 for creating a backpack checklist. Ask your child what items are needed for the activity, and work with him to create a checklist for the bag he needs to pack. Then decide where he can attach the checklist in the activity bag, and practice using it just as you have practiced using the backpack checklist: laying out the needed items, then verbally checking them off on the checklist as each item is placed in the bag. If the child often has difficulty packing needed items in an activity bag, you may want to add a goal to the HBR related to the use of an activity bag checklist.

 NEW HBR GOAL

Uses activity bag checklist(s) when packing activity bag(s).

Time Management for Daily Routines

Glitch we are battling:
Time Bandit

What it says: **"Just relax and don't worry about time passing. You'll get everything done eventually."**

Key strategy: **Time planning.**

The strategies in this section are directly related to steps introduced in Chapter 9 for time planning for school assignments. Please read Chapter 9 first for an orientation to approaches for time management.

For a child with organizational difficulties, time is a constant source of annoyance. The child is plagued by the need to get ready "in time," to get to school "on time," and to spend less time (or more time, depending on the child's personal style) getting things done. If you've followed our tips in Chapter 9 and have been working with your child on improving time estimation, using a stopwatch to time task completion, and following an afternoon schedule, your child's awareness of time may be improving. However, most children don't have a very good sense of time. They may be aware that time keeps moving, but they are not overly concerned with the units of time that pass from one point in the day to another. To test our theory, ask your nine-year-old what time she eats lunch every day at camp. She might be able to tell you that she has lunch right after swim, or that she has the third lunch period each day, but she probably can't tell you what time the lunch period starts and what time it ends. Similarly, your seven-year-old may know what time he goes to sleep each night, but he probably can't tell you how much time he needs to get ready for bed.

In Chapter 9, we've discussed how you can help your child manage time for school-related tasks more effectively, by using calendars, schedules, tracking sheets, and clocks. Your child needs to understand that the Time Bandit can also get her in trouble at home and in other regular situations (when she needs to get chores done by a certain time, get ready for school or bed, get ready to leave the house for an extracurricular activity, etc.). In these situations, the Time Bandit might tempt the child with the chance to play a favorite video game instead of sweeping under the bird's cage, distract the child with a can of shaving cream when the child is supposed to be taking a five-minute shower, or convince the child to leave homework for the last second so that there is no time to get ready for karate. The first step in helping your child get more control over regular routines is to identify how the Time Bandit interferes with the child in each problematic situation; the second step is to neutralize the Time Bandit by using time-planning strategies.

Our Time-Tested Solution: Time Planning

Just as your child has practiced time planning for homework (Chapter 9), he can learn how to plan his time better to complete regular routines efficiently. First, think about the daily routines that are problematic for your child—for instance, getting ready for school, clearing the table after eating, cleaning up her room, or taking a shower. Make a list of these problematic routines with your child, and discuss how the Time Bandit is getting in the way. The "Constructive Conversations" example below illustrates how you can start a dialogue with your child that will help you think about what's going wrong with specific daily routines and move you down a path toward creating a solution.

CONSTRUCTIVE CONVERSATIONS

Parent: I've noticed that it's been hard for you to get ready in time for school in the mornings by 7:30. Have you noticed the same thing?

Child: Yeah, I guess so. It's just so early, and I'm so tired . . .

Parent: I know. I think it's easier for the Time Bandit to get you in trouble when you're tired. How do you think the Time Bandit slows you down in the morning?

Child: Well, sometimes I stay in bed for a few minutes after my alarm goes off, and then I fall back asleep, so that slows me down. Also, when I'm tired, it's harder for me to think, and I can't figure out what to wear.

Parent: Those two Time Bandit tricks would definitely slow me down too. I've also noticed that you run out of time to eat breakfast, because it takes you such a long time to get dressed. That's pretty typical: When the Time Bandit slows us down, it also steals our free time, so we can't do the things we want to do.

Child: Yeah, I hate eating breakfast on the bus. I wish I could be ready earlier so I could relax in the morning and not be rushing all the time.

Parent: Let's think about some ways we can help you keep the Time Bandit under control in the morning, so you don't lose track of time and end up feeling stressed.

The Routine

Once you have identified which routines are problematic and how the Time Bandit interferes with the completion of those routines, you can help your child use time planning to manage each situation. First, identify a routine that you want to work on, and help your child break it down into the steps that must be completed. For example, the bedtime routine might consist of five simple steps: Shower, put clothes in hamper, get into pajamas, brush teeth, and read for 15 minutes. Make sure your child clearly understands the steps involved in the selected routine. If your child often misses steps, you may want to create a written checklist and post it somewhere visible, so that your child can check her progress as she completes the routine. For example, a checklist for the nightly routine might be posted near the child's bed or on the back of the bathroom door.

ENHANCING SUCCESS

Whenever possible, try to simplify daily routines for your child (especially younger children). The more steps are involved in a routine, the more likely your child is to leave out a step or take longer to complete the whole routine. For example, if your child has difficulty getting ready in the morning, remove the step of selecting clothes by helping your child do that the night before and leaving the clothes out on a chair. Whenever you can trim steps from a challenging routine, you will reduce stress and increase the likelihood that your child will be successful.

Next, engage your child's "time detective" by asking him first to estimate how long the whole routine should take to complete, and then to use a stopwatch for a few days to keep track of how long the routine actually takes. This will help you form a better estimate of what the ideal time for completion is and what is most realistic as an initial goal. For example, if your child takes 25–45 minutes to get ready for bed (including showering, getting dressed, brushing teeth, and laying out clothes for the next day), and you would ideally like that routine to take 20 minutes, start with a goal of 30 minutes. You can then adjust the goal for time completion (moving down to 25 and then 20 minutes gradually) as your child shows that he is able to perform more quickly. Remember: Set your child up for success when you try out a new routine, and he will be more likely to stick with it.

You will also want to brainstorm with your child a bit about how the Time Bandit might interfere with completion of the routine. For example, you might notice that your child's showers take a very long time because she tends to daydream in the shower. Ask your child if she notices the same thing, and chalk it up to the Time Bandit's interference. Then brainstorm ways for her to avoid daydreaming and stay on track in the shower. For instance, you might suggest that your child set a timer for five minutes before getting into the shower (it will be important to purchase a timer with a large enough display screen, so that your child can see the numbers counting down; another alternative tool is a waterproof shower clock, which can be attached to the shower wall). Or you might suggest that the child request a reminder from you when there are two minutes left.

Finally, help your child keep track of what time the routine must be completed and when it can be fitted into the schedule. If your child has already grown comfortable with using a Personal Calendar (see Chapter 9), this step should be familiar to him. Considering the main events that happen in a day (typical wake-up time, time the child leaves the house each day, time the child gets home, extracurricular activities, homework time, etc.), set a time period during which it makes sense for the routine to occur. The Fitting In the Steps for Daily Routines form on the following page (see the end of the Contents for information on printing copies)—which is very similar to the Afternoon Schedule bar in the Daily Assignment Record (DAR) for scheduling homework time (see Chapters 7 and 9)—can be very helpful for planning the routine. Using this form, your child can fit the steps for the routine into the schedule and record how long it actually takes to complete the routine each day (using a stopwatch or clock). Remind your child to break the routine down and write the actual steps that must be completed in each 15-minute interval on the schedule: Just as with homework planning, planning for the completion of each step (or homework assignment) will lead to more successful time management than simply writing down the ultimate goal. If the routine ends up taking longer

Fitting In the Steps for Daily Routines

Morning	After school
6:00	**3:00**
6:15	3:15
6:30	3:30
6:45	3:45
7:00	**4:00**
7:15	4:15
7:30	4:30
7:45	4:45
8:00	**5:00**
8:15	5:15
8:30	5:30
8:45	5:45
9:00	**6:00**
	6:15
	6:30
	6:45
	7:00
	7:15
	7:30
	7:45
	8:00
	8:15
	8:30
	8:45
	9:00
	9:15
	9:30
	9:45
	10:00

Did you finish on time?   _____Yes   _____No

How much extra time did the whole routine take? _____

than anticipated, this will be noted on the form, and you can discuss how the Time Bandit may have gotten in the way.

Rewarding Time Planning for Regular Routines

As with the behaviors that you've rewarded in Part III, you should adjust criteria for awarding points on the HBR as your child's capacity for success increases. When you first begin working on time planning for regular routines, you may want to reward your child for completing the Fitting In the Steps for Daily Routines form for a selected routine. As your child becomes more comfortable using the form, you can adjust the HBR goal to require timely completion of the specified routine.

 NEW HBR GOAL

Completes Fitting In the Steps for Daily Routines form for a regular routine [specify].

 NEW HBR GOAL

[Insert goal—for example, "Is ready for school"] on time.

Task Planning for Personal Goals

Glitch we are battling:
Go-Ahead-Don't-Plan Glitch

What it says: **"You don't have to plan ahead for anything. It will all work out."**

Key strategy: **Planning.**

The strategies in this section are directly related to steps introduced in Chapter 10 for planning for long-term assignments and tests. Please read Chapter 10 first for an orientation to approaches for task planning.

In Chapter 10, we've discussed the basic steps that your child needs to follow to plan appropriately for long-term school assignments and tests. We've talked about how you can help your child break down large tasks into smaller steps, identify items needed to complete each step, fit steps into the schedule, and check the final product for neatness and completeness. The same planning steps can help your child become a better planner in other areas of life as well. Once your child has mastered the steps for planning in a school context, you may want to start suggesting that your child use the same strategies in other life contexts.

Children—especially those with organizational challenges—are rarely asked to take an active role in planning for events. Usually those events are planned for them by parents. Parents usually do all the purchasing for birthday parties; make sure the house is stocked with enough snacks when a friend is going to sleep over; keep track of deadlines for after-school applications and swim meet tryouts; and make sure that their children are prepared for big events. However, the more you can teach your child at an early age about what goes into planning for events, the better your child will understand the value of planning and the steps that go into successful planning.

Our Time-Tested Solution: The Home Task-Planning Sheet

The Task-Planning Sheet was introduced in Chapter 10 as a method to help kids break large school assignments or tests into manageable steps. The version of this form provided on page 144 can be used to help your child plan for large or long-term tasks at home. Encourage your child to pull out the Home Task-Planning Sheet, or at least to go out loud through the steps on this form (listing the steps, identifying needed materials, and estimating how long each step will take), when an upcoming event or personal project requires planning. Initially, you may need to help your child identify tasks or projects that require planning and provide support in talking through the steps on the Home Task-Planning Sheet. However, with consistent encouragement and practice, your child should begin to practice planning steps more naturally.

Rewarding Task Planning

When you first begin working on task planning for personal projects, you may want to reward your child for writing down planning steps on the Home Task-Planning Sheet. As your child becomes more comfortable with the planning steps, you can adjust the HBR goal to reflect verbal consideration

Home Task-Planning Sheet

What project?		
What steps need to be taken?	**What stuff do I need?**	**How long will each step take?**

From *The Organized Child* by Richard Gallagher, Elana G. Spira, and Jennifer L. Rosenblatt. Copyright © 2018 The Guilford Press. Purchasers of this book can photocopy and/or download enlarged versions of this material (see the box at the end of the table of contents).

of the planning steps, even if the steps aren't written down on the Home Task-Planning Sheet.

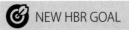 NEW HBR GOAL

Uses Home Task-Planning Sheet to plan for a personal project.

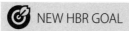 NEW HBR GOAL

Discusses task-planning steps in planning for a personal project.

Moving Forward

While we have used this chapter to address common organizational issues that arise in the home, your child may experience related challenges in other settings and situations. By tweaking any of the tools discussed above, you should be able to help your child battle the Glitches in multiple situations that demand organization. Just ask yourself some key questions: Which Glitch is tripping my child up here? Which trick is the Glitch using? What strategy can we use to put the Glitch in its place? Then you should be able to come up with some creative solutions.

In Chapter 12, we'll put it all together for you. Combining tricks and tips from Chapters 8–10 (for school-related routines) and Chapter 11 (for home routines), we'll outline steps for an organized day.

12

Putting It All Together

Making Organizational Skills Part of Your Daily Routine

By now your child has become an organizational wizard, sailing through all of life's mundane challenges. He is a list-making, paper-filing, time-planning machine and never fails to turn in homework, start a long-term assignment on the day it is assigned, dot an *i*, or cross a *t*. And you are a fount of prompting, monitoring, and praising, never missing a day of implementing the Home Behavior Record (HBR), and smiling upon your perfect child as he moves through his perfectly organized day.

Or maybe not.

While we have yet to see a child who graduates from this program as a paragon of organizational perfection, we do hope that at this point your child has made some major changes and, with continued practice, is well on her way to embedding the skills she has learned into the fabric of her everyday life. It will help her, as she moves forward, to remind her periodically of the tools she now has in her toolbox and the situations in which those tools may be helpful. In that spirit, and as a form of review, we present what a day can look like when all of the organizational skills we have discussed so far are put into action.

Morning

Child:

- Wake up and get ready, using **time planning for the morning routine** (Chapter 11).

- Pack backpack, using a **backpack checklist** (Chapter 8).
- Use the "What do I need to take to class tomorrow?" column of the **Daily Assignment Record (DAR)** for the previous day to pack anything else that needs to be taken to school (Chapter 7).

Parents:

- **Prompt** for each of these skills.
- Give **praise** for skill use.
- *Extra credit:* Create a checklist for the morning routine as a **visual reminder.**

At School

Child:

- Use a **locker checklist** (if applicable; Chapter 8) to see what can be stored in the locker and what needs to be taken to class.
- Store items in the locker, using a **locker shelf** (Chapter 8).
- Use the "What is the homework?" column of the **DAR** (Chapter 7) to write down homework.
- Transfer long-term assignments and tests to the **Assignment and Test Calendar** (Chapter 7).
- Store papers in an **accordion file** (Chapter 8).
- Store pencils and other items in **containers and compartments** (Chapter 8).
- Use a **locker checklist** (if applicable) between classes to see what is needed for the afternoon (Chapter 8).
- Consult the **backpack checklist** (Chapter 8) and the "What do I need to take home?" column of the **DAR** (Chapter 7) when packing up to go home.

After School: Homework Time

Child:

- Get work area **"Ready to Go"** (Chapter 9).
- Check the "Tests and long-term assignments" column of the **DAR** for any new long-term assignments or tests (or transfer them over now, if there was no time at school; Chapter 7).

- Plan for any long-term assignments, using the **Task-Planning Sheet** (Chapter 10).

- Write down steps for any long-term assignments or tests on the **Assignment and Test Calendar** (Chapter 10).

- Check the "What is the homework?" column of the **DAR** for tonight's homework (Chapter 7).

- Plan the afternoon and evening with the **Afternoon Schedule** and **Personal Calendar** (Chapter 9).

- **"Check It Out"** to make sure work is done neatly and completely (Chapter 10).

- **"Weed It Out"** and put papers in the **hanging file box** for long-term storage (Chapter 8).

Parents:

- **Prompt** for each of these skills.

- Give **praise** for skill use.

- *Extra credit:* Post a **visual reminder** of the homework rules in the space where your child works.

After School: Everything Else

Child:

- Use an **activity bag checklist** (Chapter 11) to pack for after-school activities.

- Use **storage containers** (Chapter 11) to organize toys and games when playing.

- Use **time planning** (Chapter 11) for the evening routine.

Parents:

- **Prompt** for each of these skills.

- Give **praise** for skill use.

- Award **points** for skill use on the HBR.

- Give your child any **rewards** he has earned from his HBR.

- Check the Mastery Worksheet to see if your child has mastered any skills and if a new goal should be added to the HBR.

- *Extra credit:* Make a checklist for the evening routine as a **visual reminder.**

Helping Your Child Maintain Good Organizational Skills

By prompting, monitoring, praising, and rewarding your child, you have played a crucial role in helping her learn important organizational, time management, and planning (OTMP) skills. However, once your child has mastered these skills, you want to make sure that she continues to use them without becoming overly dependent on prompts and rewards. After all, you won't be there in the college dorm to remind your child to clear off her desk, pack her things for class, or plan for an upcoming exam . . . or to give her a reward if she does so! Do not fear: You can continue motivating your child, while cutting back on reminders and rewards, using procedures that we call "fading" and "thinning." Fading means reducing how often you give prompts, and thinning means reducing how often you reward.

Fading: Reducing How Often You Prompt

The ideal goal is for your child to use organizational tools and routines without always having to be reminded to do so. Reducing how often you prompt gives your child opportunities to become self-reliant and to use organizational skills when needed. This will also help your child learn more quickly to recognize situations that call for OTMP skills and to use them even when you are not there.

There is no "one right" fading schedule. Deciding how to fade prompting with your child will depend on three factors:

■ *How often you currently remind your child to use OTMP skills.* If you have to provide near-constant prompts to get your child through the daily routines, you will have to cut back on those prompts gradually.

■ *How well your child does when prompts are not given.* If you have experimented with cutting back on prompts already, and your child does just fine, you can probably reduce prompts at a faster rate.

■ *Your child's ongoing organizational strengths and weaknesses.* Think about which situations require more or fewer prompts to ensure success; you may be able to fade certain prompts more quickly than others. For example, your child may manage time for daily assignments well, but may need more prompts to get long-term projects done in time.

With these factors in mind, you can begin the process of reducing (fading) the number of prompts you give your child:

1. Let your child know that you will be reducing how often you provide reminders to be organized, and explain why you are doing this.

2. Discuss with your child how visual or written cues can be useful reminders to use skills and stay organized, instead of relying on your prompts. For example, point out how your child can use a backpack checklist as a prompt to make sure that all materials have been packed. You may want to come up with some additional visual cues to replace your verbal reminders (such as a sign above the homework desk that reads, "Don't forget to use the Afternoon Schedule before you start working!").

3. Keep track of what happens when you don't give prompts. Does your child carry out or fail to carry out the required skill? Use this information to decide which prompts to fade and when. For example, if you notice that materials have been left out of the backpack, you might have to go back to regularly prompting your child to check that everything has been packed.

4. When your child independently uses an OTMP skill, praise your child for having done so without being reminded.

Thinning: Reducing How Often You Reward

In Chapter 5 we've discussed why providing concrete, immediate rewards is so valuable for motivating the use of new organizational skills. However, you cannot and should not provide such rewards forever. Here are some strategies for thinning rewards:

1. Increase the **length of time** before your child is rewarded for being well organized. For example, instead of giving your child a reward every day that the DAR is completed, signed by the teacher, and brought home, reward your child at the end of the week if the DAR was completed and signed on at least four days, and give a "bonus" if the DAR was completed and signed every day. *Remember to praise* your child each day for having brought home a completed and signed DAR.

2. Increase the **number of times** your child has to show good organizational skills before being rewarded. For example, instead of giving a reward each day that your child shows good time management for homework,

wait to give the reward until your child has shown this on three occasions. Remember to praise, hug, or give a high five to your child each day good management of homework time happens. To keep track of when to give a reward, you can continue to record your child's behavior on a simple chart, like the HBR. The chart can also remind you to praise your child for using organizational tools and routines.

Remember that even though concrete rewards should be thinned out over time, you should continue to give praise and social rewards (high five, hug, pat on the back) when your child shows organized behavior. You may not remember to praise your child every time he uses an organizational skill, but try to do so as often as you can. Even a few simple words—"Wow, your backpack has been at the door, all packed up, this whole week," "You did an amazing job getting all of those assignments done tonight," or "You are using your planner so consistently these days!"—can make a huge difference in keeping your child motivated to stay on top of organizational tasks and demands.

13

When Your Child Needs
Additional Help

As we have said throughout this book, we never expect a child to have developed absolutely perfect, error-free organizational skills by the end of the Organizational Skills Training (OST) program. We do, however, expect a child to be making major changes—that is, to be forming new habits, showing improved school performance, and experiencing less stress. (We also expect, as a by-product, that the family's stress level is significantly decreasing.) If you have worked diligently through the program and are not seeing these types of results, it is time to consider seeking further help. Common scenarios in which a family can benefit from professional help include the following:

1. **Your child has, or you suspect your child may have, a clinical diagnosis.** As described below in more detail, if your child has attention-deficit/hyperactivity disorder (ADHD, the most common diagnosis for children struggling with significant organizational deficits) or another complicating diagnosis, she should be seen by a professional. While the techniques outlined in this book are consistent with the gold-standard approach for treating organizational deficits in children with clinical diagnoses, the guidance of an experienced practitioner in implementing these techniques is warranted in more severe and/or complex cases. Furthermore, if you suspect that your child may be struggling with feelings of anxiety or depression, or may be falling behind in school because of a learning problem, you should consult with a mental health professional to ensure that those important issues are addressed (see below for more information on seeking help).

2. **Your child has so strongly internalized negative messages about his organizational failures that he has lost motivation to change.** It is hard to spend so many years struggling with an issue that too many people brand as a character flaw, whether they call it "laziness," "poor work ethic," or "carelessness." This is an unfair casting of a true skill deficit—and, unfortunately, it is all too common for children with organizational skills deficits to buy into these characterizations and believe that they are incapable of change. We see this particularly in older children, for whom the negative impact of these messages has built up over time. A professional can help these children better understand the true nature of their organizational challenges and work with them to reverse their negative self-perceptions, giving them the confidence they need to take on the task of building their organizational skills.

3. **The parent–child relationship is strained.** It is difficult to find a relationship between a parent and a child struggling with organizational skills that is *not* strained. All of the nagging, the struggles over homework, and the repeated night-before-the-due-date crises can take their toll. As a parent, it is important to take a step back and determine if this (or some stressor coming from an entirely separate part of your relationship) is making it too hard to work through this program on your own. Sometimes a neutral third party is necessary to make the program work.

Assessing for ADHD

If you believe your child may have symptoms of ADHD, you should seek out a full evaluation from a mental health professional or pediatric specialist with experience with ADHD to determine whether your child meets the diagnostic criteria for the disorder. This evaluation will help determine whether high levels of inattention and hyperactivity/impulsivity are present and impairing, and occur in at least two settings. The evaluator will ask you for detailed information about your child's functioning at home, and will also seek information from your child's teacher to determine how your child is functioning in school. The evaluation will likely include a diagnostic interview and information from rating scales that you and the teacher (and, possibly, your child) will complete, along with a detailed psychosocial history and general medical clearance. A thorough evaluation for ADHD is critical to rule out alternative explanations for inattention and hyperactivity/impulsivity, and to structure an appropriate treatment plan that will help manage your child's symptoms.

If your child is diagnosed with ADHD and also has organizational skills difficulties, your therapist may recommend the OST program as an adjunct to behavior therapy and/or medication. But if your child with ADHD is not responding to the strategies that you have tried from this book, an experienced behavior therapist may be able to help you get the treatment on track by providing additional structure and support. Even if you get assistance from a therapist in conducting OST with your child, you will not have wasted your time reading this book. As we have emphasized before, OST requires a parent to play an active role in supporting a child's use of organizational skills. The tips and techniques that you have learned by reading this book will help you work with your child and your child's therapist to improve your child's organizational skills.

Assessing for Other Diagnoses

While ADHD is the most common diagnosis associated with organizational skills difficulties, there are other clinical issues that can affect your child's functioning. Some of these may require immediate attention before skills training should be undertaken, and may complicate attempts to conduct OST. The following brief descriptions provide an overview of some common diagnoses that often accompany ADHD and may be related to organizational skills deficits—but if you're concerned that your child may be experiencing any of these symptoms, please consult a children's mental health professional for an assessment.

If your child is experiencing significant emotional issues, such as anxiety or depression, you should consult with a therapist to determine whether it would be more appropriate to address those concerns before initiating OST. Anxiety disorders, found in up to 25% of children with ADHD, can complicate the delivery of OST by causing children to worry about reaching point goals for skill use. You and your child's therapist should consider how your child has reacted in the past to monitoring/point systems (if any such systems have been used), and adjust the OST system accordingly. For example, you may need to ensure that points earned in the behavior management system are tied to bonus activities and prizes, rather than your child's typical privileges. Otherwise, your child may spend excessive amounts of time worrying about losing privileges, instead of focusing on organizational tasks.

Children with significant obsessive–compulsive patterns may also find OST anxiety-provoking, but for another reason: They will be asked to follow specific routines, and in some cases the routines could become compulsive in nature, resulting in heightened anxiety rather than improved functioning. Furthermore, if your child has obsessive–compulsive disorder (OCD), you and your child's therapist may need to consider to what extent the child's obsessions and compulsions may account for OTMP deficits, especially in time management. A child may be very slow in meeting time goals and deadlines because of the need to perform compulsive actions in response to obsessive worries. If so, using the skills in this book to try to improve the child's time management may not work, as the child may experience too much distress in changing compulsive behaviors. Instead, the underlying obsessive–compulsive cycle will probably need to be addressed. We have used OST successfully to improve organizational skills in children with OCD; however, we would suggest that you work on these skills with your child in consultation with your child's therapist.

If your child has a significant learning disorder or language disorder, or has borderline or lower intellectual functioning, the OST program may need to be adapted in terms of presentation and pace. For example, a child with a receptive language disorder may have difficulty comprehending verbal explanations and discussions, such as those we recommend for introducing a new organizational skill/routine. In this situation, you should adapt the suggested dialogues to make them shorter and more focused—using words that your child can understand, and speaking at a slower pace so your child has more time to process the content. A speech or language specialist can provide concrete recommendations for communicating effectively with a child who has receptive language difficulties.

Learning disorders, particularly reading disorders and writing disorders, are quite common in children who have ADHD, with rates of overlap between 20 and 45%. If your child has been diagnosed with a learning disorder and requires tutoring or special education services, you may want to involve your child's support team in helping you adapt and deliver the program in this book so that it is most effective for your child. The services that your child receives in school may also affect how she completes some of the organizational routines covered in this book. For example, if your child qualifies for a special education itinerant teacher (SEIT) in school, the SEIT may help her write down homework assignments and pack her bag. If so, you will want to discuss with your SEIT how to give your child opportunities to perform manageable tasks in the school context. If your child has a writing disorder, writing down homework assignments on the DAR may be difficult; you may need to modify the form so that your child has more room to write, or has more opportunities to circle options as opposed to writing them in. If your child has a math learning disability, she may have particular difficulties with the time management portion of our program. You may need to work with a tutor to provide additional instruction in time telling and support in recording time estimates and calculations of how much time has passed.

When there is a general problem in learning related to below-average intellectual functioning, you may encounter a number of challenges in working through the organizational strategies in this book. If your child has significant impairments in processing speed and memory, verbal review of skills and practice of new skills are likely to take more time than we've described. A learning professional should be able to provide consultation in best practices for modifying verbal presentations and optimizing memory of routines.

Oppositional defiant disorder (ODD), which involves a persistent pattern of anger, irritability, arguing, and defiance toward parents and other authority figures, is very common in children with ADHD (approximately 50–60% of cases). Serious conduct disorder, recognized as a persistent pattern of behavior in which the rights of others or basic social rules are violated, is present in a significant minority (20%). If your child has severe problems with conduct, those will clearly take priority over addressing organizational skills difficulties. However, we have implemented OST with children with ODD, both as part of the research trial for the program and in general clinical practice. In general, you will need to consider how frequent and severe your child's oppositional behaviors are before you decide whether to start OST. If your child is constantly and significantly oppositional at home (throwing severe tantrums, refusing to comply with all requests, physically fighting with siblings, etc.), you should consult with a behavior therapist for parent training to manage oppositionality before you start working with your child on organized behaviors. Because the OST program relies on a cooperative effort between parents and children, it is unlikely to succeed if a child is excessively oppositional and a parent has not mastered general behavior management strategies.

Symptoms of autism spectrum disorder (ASD) should also be considered before OST is implemented. Two common patterns in ASD may affect the success of the OST program: rigidity in routines, and lack of interest in accepting social conventions. A child with ASD who has rigid organizational routines may be unwilling to change responses to organizational situations, even if the current routines are not successful. Furthermore, a child with ASD who does not agree with social conventions, such as the importance of school success, may not be invested in learning more effective ways to handle school demands. In both situations, motivating the child to change behaviors or become invested in school success might not be possible without prior extensive work. We have successfully used OST to improve organizational functioning in children with ASD symptoms, when those symptoms were relatively mild. If your child experiences severe ASD symptoms and displays considerable rigidity and little interest in accepting social conventions, you will likely need to work with a therapist to help your child improve organizational skills.

The success of any endeavor depends on a careful consideration of context and a willingness to be flexible in adapting to multiple factors. The reason you are reading this book is that your child needs help to become more organized. However, as we have just discussed, disorganization can occur in the context of any of several serious mental health issues. You may need to consult with a mental health or learning professional to obtain additional support in addressing your child's larger behavioral/learning issues, or to help you adapt the OST program to best suit your child's specific needs. The Resources section near the end of this book lists sources of more assistance for the concerns raised in this chapter.

How to Find Help

When seeking a professional to help your family, you should focus on two criteria: the professional's credentials, and her training in empirically supported treatments for organizational skills deficits. In regard to credentials, look for a licensed psychologist, psychiatrist, or social worker who specializes in the treatment of children and who has expertise in cognitive-behavioral therapy. "Cognitive-behavioral therapy" is a broad term for a school of therapy that addresses maladaptive thoughts and behaviors. All treatments that have shown efficacy for addressing organizational skills deficits in clinical trials thus far fall under the umbrella of cognitive-behavioral therapy.

There are seven specific cognitive-behavioral programs that have good evidence behind them for the treatment of organizational skills difficulties. They are listed in the box on the following page. It should be noted that all of these programs were tested exclusively on children with ADHD. Unfortunately, to the best of our knowledge, no organizational skills programs have been well studied in children without ADHD.

If you are able to find a professional trained in one of these programs, this is unquestionably your best option. Unfortunately, such professionals are few and far between. If you live in the general vicinity of one of the

Evidence-Based Treatment Programs
for Organizational Skills Deficits

Organizational Skills Training (OST). Developed by Howard B. Abikoff, PhD, and Richard Gallagher, PhD, of the New York University (NYU) Child Study Center at Langone Medical Center.

- Treatment that forms the basis for this book.

Parents and Teachers Helping Kids Organize (PATHKO). Developed by Karen Wells, PhD, of Duke University; Desiree Murray, PhD, of the University of North Carolina, Chapel Hill; and Richard Gallagher, PhD, and Howard B. Abikoff, PhD (see above).

- Treatment focused on training parents and teachers to implement behavioral reward systems that motivate children to improve their organizational skills.

Homework, Organizational Skills, and Planning (HOPS). Developed by Joshua Langberg, PhD, of Virginia Commonwealth University.

- School-based program focused on teaching, monitoring, and rewarding organizational systems, homework management, and time management/planning.

Challenging Horizons Program (CHP). Developed by Steven W. Evans, PhD, of Ohio University.

- A broader after-school program targeting school, social, and family functioning in middle school students with ADHD; includes modules dedicated to organizational skills.

Child Life and Attention Skills (CLAS). Developed by Linda Pfiffner, PhD, of the University of California, San Francisco School of Medicine.

- Program with parent, child, and teacher components targeting a range of problems (including organizational problems) common to children with the inattentive subtype of ADHD.

Cognitive-Behavioral Therapy for Adults with ADHD. Developed by Mary V. Solanto of the NYU Child Study Center at Langone Medical Center.

- Adult treatment that teaches OTMP strategies, as well as addressing maladaptive cognitions that interfere with self-management. Appropriate for college-age students.

Parent–Teen Therapy for Executive Function Deficits and ADHD. Developed by Margaret Sibley, PhD, of Florida International University.

- A clinical program for parents and teens to improve motivation and organizational skills.

research centers associated with these programs, try contacting them to see if they can refer you to a professional in your area. If not, a professional with a solid background in child cognitive-behavioral therapy is your next best bet. If you live in the United States or Canada, the Association for Cognitive and Behavioral Therapies (ABCT; *www.abct.org*) is a good resource for finding a cognitive-behavioral therapist in your area.

Can Medication Help?

If your child has ADHD, medication may also be useful in addressing his organizational skills deficits. For about 40% of children with ADHD, stimulant medication can significantly improve organizational skills without any other intervention. For other children with ADHD, adding medication to improve attention and behavior control may make it easier to learn and use organizational skills. Other medications may also be useful in addressing anxiety that may contribute to or complicate organizational issues.

If you are "on the fence" about medication, most professionals are happy to schedule a consultation to discuss the pros and cons and answer questions before you make a decision. We recommend seeking out a child psychiatrist or child psychopharmacologist. While many primary care doctors will prescribe medication for ADHD, the road to finding the right medication often involves trials of more than one medication and dosage to determine the optimal treatment for your child. The knowledge and experience of a specialist can be very helpful in navigating this journey.

Don't Give Up!

It can be (mind-numbingly) frustrating when you expend a great deal of time and energy trying to address an already frustrating problem and don't get the results you hoped for. As tempting as it is to throw in the towel, you owe it to your child to exhaust all the options for help that are out there. Organizational skills deficits tend not to magically correct themselves, even as your child matures into adulthood. And they are required for success in almost any field. The goal of all this work is to prevent your child's organizational skills deficits from clouding her ability to show all of her gifts and talents to the world. If this book is just the first step on your journey, then we hope it gives you the knowledge and the impetus to move on to the next step, and (if necessary) the next, until your child finds success.

Appendix

Creating Your Own Planner

You can make planners for your child at home, using a folder. You'll need to make a new one of these every three months, but you'll have to replenish some of the components every month, as described below. You can also make a larger, sturdier version at a copy center; complete instructions are available online (see the box at the end of the Contents).

You will need the following materials for every three months (see the end of the Contents for information on downloading and printing the copies you'll need for the planner):

- 1 thick, two-pocket folder.
- 75 copies of the Daily Assignment Record (DAR), printed in landscape orientation (see Chapter 7). Staple only 25 of these pages (one month's worth) into the folder at a time, since that's all that will fit easily, and then replenish these at the end of the month.
- 3 copies of the Assignment and Test Calendar (see Chapter 7), also printed in landscape orientation. Fill in the month and days for each copy before you staple it into the folder.
- 1 Personal Calendar card, printed on card stock and cut to size.
- 10 copies of the Task-Planning Sheet (see Chapter 10).

Assemble as follows:

1. Staple the DAR pages on the right side of the folder.
2. On the left side of the folder, staple the three Assignment and Test

Calendar pages. Put the current month on top, with the next two months underneath.

3. Staple the Personal Calendar card to the folder pocket underneath the Assignment and Test Calendar pages.

4. Put the Task-Planning Sheet pages in the left-hand pocket.

The completed planner should look like this when the folder is opened up. Place staples where indicated by the arrows.

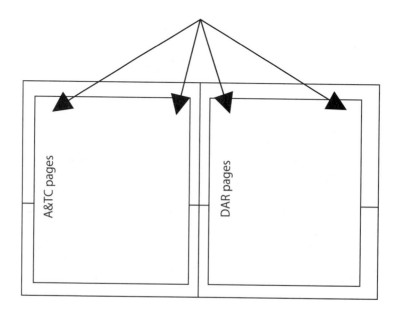

Resources

Books

If your child's organizational difficulties are related to ADHD and/or another behavioral or emotional disorder, you may want more detailed, in-depth information on these disorders and the parenting challenges they can create. These books (some of which were written for professionals, but may be of interest for those seeking comprehensive information) also provide more on using behavior management strategies to motivate improved behavior in the various domains of everyday life.

For Parents

Barkley, R. A. (2013). *Taking Charge of ADHD: The Complete, Authoritative Guide for Parents* (3rd ed.). New York: Guilford Press.

Barkley, R. A., & Benton, C. M. (2013). *Your Defiant Child: 8 Steps to Better Behavior* (2nd ed.). New York: Guilford Press.

Barkley, R. A., & Robin, A. L., with Benton, C. M. (2014). *Your Defiant Teen: 10 Steps to Resolve Conflict and Rebuild Your Relationship* (2nd ed.). New York: Guilford Press.

Dawson, P. & Guare, R. (2009). *Smart but Scattered: The Revolutionary "Executive Skills" Approach to Helping Kids Reach Their Potential.* New York: Guilford Press.

Dawson, P. & Guare, R. (2012). *Smart but Scattered Teens: The "Executive Skills" Program for Helping Teens Reach Their Potential.* New York: Guilford Press.

Dawson, P. & Guare, R. (2017). *The Work Smart Academic Planner (Revised Edition): Write It Down, Get It Done.* New York: Guilford Press.

Greene, R. W. (2001). *The Explosive Child: A New Approach for Understanding and*

Parenting Easily Frustrated, Chronically Inflexible Children. New York: Harper-Collins.

Kazdin, A. E. (2008). *The Kazdin Method for Parenting the Defiant Child*. New York: Houghton Mifflin Harcourt.

For Professionals

Barkley, R. A. (2015). *Attention-Deficit Hyperactivity Disorder: A Handbook for Diagnosis and Treatment* (4th ed.). New York: Guilford Press.

DuPaul, G. J., & Stoner, G. (2014). *ADHD in the Schools: Assessment and Intervention Strategies* (3rd ed.). New York: Guilford Press.

Mash, E. J., & Barkley, R. A. (Eds.). (2014). *Child Psychopathology* (3rd ed.). New York: Guilford Press.

Robin, A. T. (1998). *ADHD in Adolescents: Diagnosis and Treatment*. New York: Guilford Press.

Treatment Programs

These books outline treatment programs targeting executive function difficulties in children, teens, and adults.

Gallagher, R., Abikoff, H. B., & Spira, E. G. (2014). *Organizational Skills Training for Children with ADHD: An Empirically Supported Treatment*. New York: Guilford Press.

Power, T., Karustis, J. L., & Habboushe, D. F. (2001). *Homework Success for Children with ADHD: A Family-School Intervention Program*. New York: Guilford Press.

Sibley, M. H. (2017). *Parent–Teen Therapy for Executive Function Deficits and ADHD: Building Skills and Motivation*. New York: Guilford Press.

Solanto, M. V. (2011). *Cognitive-Behavioral Therapy for Adult ADHD: Targeting Executive Dysfunction*. New York: Guilford Press.

For Children

The following books and series provide user-friendly steps to help children work on self-control, emotion regulation, anxiety, and organizationwith parents' help.

Fox, J. (2017) *Getting Organized Without Losing It (Laugh and Learn)*. Minneapolis, MN: Free Spirit.

Huebner, D. (2006). *What to Do When You Worry Too Much: A Kid's Guide to Overcoming Anxiety*. Washington, DC: Magination Press.

Huebner, D. (2006). *What to Do When You Grumble Too Much: A Kid's Guide to Overcoming Negativity.* Washington, DC: Magination Press.

Huebner, D. (2007). *What to Do When Your Brain Gets Stuck: A Kid's Guide to Overcoming OCD.* Washington, DC: Magination Press.

Huebner, D. (2008). *What to Do When Your Temper Flares: A Kid's Guide to Overcoming Problems with Anger.* Washington, DC: Magination Press.

Shapiro, L. (2010). *The ADHD Workbook for Kids: Helping Children Gain Self-Confidence, Social Skills, and Self-Control.* Oakland, CA: Instant Help Books.

Periodicals

ADDitude: Strategies and Support for ADHD and LD (online and print periodical) is an excellent source of useful information about ADHD and learning disabilities, covering a wide range of topics. *www.additudemag.com*

The ADHD Report (edited by R. A. Barkley, published by The Guilford Press) is a newsletter designed for clinicians who want to remain current in the scientific and clinical literature on ADHD. Parents of children with ADHD may also find the content useful. *www.guilford.com/journals/The-ADHD-Report/Russell-Barkley/10658025*

Attention Magazine is the official publication of Children and Adults with ADHD (CHADD), the largest national support organization for ADHD. *www.chadd.org*

CHADD Newsletter is a newsletter for parents of children with ADHD and adults with ADHD who are members of CHADD. *http://chadd.org/Understanding-ADHD/About-ADHD/ADHD-Weekly*

Websites for Interested Nonprofessionals

AboutKidsHealth (*www.aboutkidshealth.ca*), developed by The Hospital for Sick Children in Toronto, is a valuable source of information on child health, behavior, and development.

Autism Research Institute (*www.autism.com*) provides research-based information to parents and professionals around the world on the diagnosis and treatment of autism.

CHADD (*www.chadd.org*) is an organization dedicated to providing advocacy, education, and support for individuals with ADHD, as indicated above. The website is an excellent resource for parents and professionals on topics related to ADHD. The website also houses the National Resource Center on ADHD, which provides specific information on scientifically sound practices for managing ADHD.

Child Mind Institute (*https://childmind.org*) provides a wide range of articles on topics related to child mental health, behavior, and development.

Child Study Center at NYU Langone Medical Center (www.nyulangone.org/locations/child-study-center) provides a number of brief articles on the development, adjustment, and treatment of children, teens, and young adults.

LD OnLine (www.ldonline.org) provides up-to-date information and advice about learning disabilities and ADHD.

National Center for Learning Disabilities (www.ncld.org) is a nonprofit organization that provides resources for helping children, parents, teachers, and others understand the challenges and successes experienced by people with learning disabilities and attention disorders.

Understood (www.understood.org) is a website affiliated with the National Center for Learning Disabilities and maintained specifically for parents.

Wrightslaw (www.wrightslaw.com) contains articles focusing on special education law and advocacy for children with disabilities, including information on individualized educational programs (IEPs) and Section 504 accommodations.

Websites for Professional Organizations and Governmental Resources

United States and Canada

These sites contain resources for parents of children with organizational problems and for adults with such problems, as well as for professionals. Their content is likely to be well informed by research.

American Academy of Child and Adolescent Psychiatry (www.aacap.org) is the professional organization in the United States for psychiatrists who have had extended training in child and adolescent evaluation and treatment. The website contains a number of articles on child and adolescent conditions, as well as a link for finding a child and adolescent psychiatrist in your area.

American Academy of Pediatrics (www.aap.org) is the professional organization for U.S. pediatricians. The website has a large section of information for parents on aspects of children's health, development, and illnesses/other conditions, including behavioral and emotional problems.

American Psychological Association (www.apa.org) is the professional organization for psychologists in the United States. The Psychology Help Center provides a means for finding a psychologist and contains a section of articles on family and relationships.

Association for Behavioral and Cognitive Therapies (www.abct.org) is a professional organization for psychologists, psychiatrists, social workers, marriage and family counselors, and mental health counselors who specialize in the use of behavioral and cognitive therapy approaches. The site contains articles on important mental health topics. There is also a means of finding a therapist in your area.

Canadian Academy of Child and Adolescent Psychiatry/Académie Canadienne de

Psychiatrie de l'Enfant et de l'Adolescent (www.cacap-acpea.org) is the professional organization for child and adolescent psychiatrists in Canada. Like its U.S. counterpart, AACAP (see above), it is a source of information for families.

Canadian Psychological Association/Société Canadienne de Psychologie (www.cpa. ca) is the professional organization for psychologists in Canada. The website contains a resource center that tells how to find a psychologist and includes a number of fact sheets on various conditions in children, teens, and adults.

Centers for Disease Control and Prevention (www.cdc.gov), a major branch of the U.S. Department of Health and Human Services, is dedicated to the preservation of health and safety in the United States. The website contains an alphabetical listing of conditions, with information on the nature of those conditions and how they are evaluated and treated. Child and adolescent behavioral and emotional disorders are among the conditions reviewed.

Ministries of Education (Canada): Individual sites for each province. In each Canadian province, the ministry of education has a website that provides resources for families about topical issues in education, as well as content that guides families on enhancing the achievement and adjustment of their children.

National Association of School Psychologists (www.nasponline.org/resources-and-publications/families-and-educators) is a professional organization for school psychologists in the United States and several other countries. This particular link on the general NASP website contains information on facilitating achievement and adjustment in school for all children, as well as discussions of issues that children demonstrate in school.

National Education Association (www.nea.org) is a professional organization for teachers in the United States. The website contains resources for parents that address homework issues, tips for helping children succeed in school, and many other topics.

National Institute of Mental Health (www.nimh.nih.gov) is one of the National Institutes of Health. Among many other resources, the website provides readings on a variety of mental health conditions, and describes the process of getting help for mental illness.

National Parent Teacher Association (www.pta.org) is a network including not only parents and teachers, but also students, administrators, and leaders in businesses and communities. The website contains a variety of guides for parents that foster school success.

Other Countries

Child and Adolescent Mental Health (www.camh.org.uk) is an information source for professionals, young people, and parents, based in the United Kingdom.

Department of Health, Australian Government (www.health.gov.au), maintains a website that contains many articles on child and adolescent mental health and a listing of resources for mental health services.

New Zealand Psychological Association (www.psychology.org.nz) is the professional organization for psychologists in New Zealand. The "Community" tab offers practical advice on discipline practices, as well as links for obtaining child mental health and family services.

Psychological Society of Ireland (www.psihq.ie) is the professional organization for psychologists in Ireland. The website provides a link for finding a psychologist in Ireland. It also offers Psychology Matters, a series of tips for mental health and well-being. Links for adults and youth, based on content from the Health Services Executive, are provided at another site *(www.yourmentalhealth.ie).*

Royal Australian and New Zealand College of Psychiatrists (www.ranzcp.org) is the professional organization for psychiatrists in Australia and New Zealand. A "Mental Health Advice" tab on this website provides fact sheets on conditions and treatment information.

Tools

MotivAider (www.habitchange.com) is a device or app that privately provides a person with a vibrating stimulus that can be a reminder to keep paying attention. It can be set to provide reminders at different intervals. The application was one of the winners of the Best ADHD App award in 2016 from Healthline *(www.healthline.com).*

Work-Smart Academic Planner (www.guilford.com/books/The-Work-Smart-Academic-Planner/Dawson-Guare/9781462530205) is a planner that incorporates pages to assist in tracking assignments, managing materials, and planning. It contains some aspects of the Daily Assignment Record and other forms for the planner described in this book.

Index

Note. *f* or *t* following a page number indicates a figure or a table.

About the Authors

Richard Gallagher, PhD, Elana G. Spira, PhD, and **Jennifer L. Rosenblatt, PhD,** serve on the faculty of the Child Study Center, part of Hassenfeld Children's Hospital at New York University Langone Health. With decades of combined experience working with children with a range of learning and behavior challenges, they participated in developing and testing Organizational Skills Training, the program on which this book is based.